Northumberland Place - Names

by

STAN BECKENSALL

B.A.(Hons), Dip.Ed.

First published by Frank Graham, 1975
Published by Butler Publishing, 1992

I.S.B.N. 0 946928 41 X

Butler Publishing
Thropton, Rothbury. NE65 7LP

Printed by:
The Abbey Press
Hexham, Northumberland. NE46 1PG

CONTENTS

Glanton ½
Prendwick 5
Alnham 6¼
Coldstream 24
A697
Shawdon Hall ¾
Titlington 3
Bolton 2
Powburn 1½
Wooler 10

INTRODUCTION

The purpose of this book is to make available a comprehensive guide to Northumberland place-names. It is not original, as the spade-work has been done in two main works:

(1) The Place-Names of Northumberland and Durham, by Professor Allen Mawer (Cambridge U.P., 1920).

(2) The Concise Oxford Dictionary of English Place-Names (Fourth Edition) Eilert Ekwall.

As the first is long out of print and the second a very large and wide-ranging survey, the need for such a book is clear. To help the general reader, only the earliest spelling of a name has been included and the complicated detail given by Dr. Mawer has been excluded. A map divided into regions is included to locate places fairly easily.

I am pleased that this book has been reprinted, as people are happy to have something easily portable for pocket or car, and are interested in what place-names mean, once they are made aware that the often strange and apparently inexplicable names seen on signposts and maps have an origin rooted so deeply in the past.

It has not been possible to re-write the book, but I should like to offer Barley Valley for Bardon Mill to those who noticed that I'd missed it out and told me so.

One aspect of the pursuit of name-meanings has been the recording of Field Names, and the consideration of what they mean and how they have developed. This is a fascinating task, and the recording is something that anyone can do. I am pleased that my Northumberland Field Names, printed in 1977 helped many people in their research, for that was my first venture into the reasons why all our fields have names, and why they change so frequently.

Many of our personal names originate from names (my first name and surname, for example, and names like Shaftoe and Bolam are just two examples of people named after places.

A warning: There is no end to study of names. Once you start, you may not be able to give it up!

The Place-Names of Northumberland

For study purposes place-names are split up into ELEMENTS. For example, FORD is a single element, and means exactly what it says. Alnwick has two elements: ALN-WICK, the first being a pre-Roman river name and the second meaning settlement or farm. STAMFORDHAM has three elements which mean stony-ford-settlement.

It is no use guessing what a place-name means. The first step is to find out its earliest form of spelling, and this comes from old documents. Dictionaries of place-names give not only the earliest spellings, but any subsequent changes. One example will serve to show what can happen:

> **Ashington** in 1205 was spelt *Essenden* in the Curia Regis, or king's court, Rolls. In 1242 the word was Essingden in "The Book of Fees".

It is clear then that "ton", which looks like *tun,* meaning a settlement, was not the original ending, but *denu,* meaning a valley. At first sight "Ashing" – looks like the kind of Anglo-Saxon construction that means 'the people of' some Saxon personal name, but the original spelling shows that it comes from aescen (ash trees). So the old spelling suggests that Ashington was a valley in which many ash trees grew.

From the same example we can see that not only spelling changes, but so does pronunciation. Ess is changed to Ash.

The way in which a name is pronounced locally is important, and as a general rule it would be better if a place-name were spelt as it is pronounced. Nothing could be more unhelpful than the spelling Ulgham, when it is pronounced Uffm. However, sometimes people within a very small area can pronounce a place-name differently, which adds another complication.

Even with early spellings it is not always clear what a name means. Sometimes the solution may lie in a close study of local land forms – valleys, burns, bends in a river, vegetation. Almost all Northumbrian place-names came into being with the Anglo-Saxon invaders, and you can see the kind of conditions that they faced. The earliest "Old English" names point to family groupings, where the leader brought his people and gave his name to the family settlement.

For example, Aedwulf's people settled in the northern part of the county and gave their name to **Eglingham.** The names of so many of these settlers are locked up inside place-names. Occasionally it is not easy to distinguish between a personal name and any other, because nicknames can develop from all kinds of sources.

Naturally, a place can also be located by some local feature: the bend in a stream, the junction of two streams, a deep valley, round hill, thick forest, etc. There may be badgers, deer, foxes or other animals in large numbers, to give a place its name. A settler may have to clear away forest, leaving rough ground or a glade, or an enclosure for his beasts, or he may build a house on the clearing. All these things may be recorded. One can see that the Anglo-Saxon settlers were forest clearers and agriculturalists.

Some names go back to a time before the collapse of the Roman Empire. The pre-Roman people of this country (known variously as Celtic, British, etc.) had their own place-names, but few have survived. In Northumberland the Roman conquest north of Hadrian's Wall would not have been complete, and people would have lived without much interference from Rome – yet not much of their survival is reflected in the names.

The Roman language was wiped out, it seems, and the preponderance of Latin in our language comes from the Norman French. Yet there are some elements that are from Roman Northumberland – the Wall has left its mark, and so have the "Chesters" scattered around.

So the Anglo-Saxons remain the greatest influence on our place-names. Despite their defeat by William and his Normans, there is little French influence. There are direct imports like **Blanchland** and **Guyzance,** but the main influence of the Normans was on spelling. Imagine the educated Norman scribes touring Saxon villages for the Domesday Book Survey trying to turn Saxon sounds of places into the nearest phonetic equivalent in Norman French! We have no Domesday Book for Northumberland, but we have inherited some of the spelling problems.

Names remain a source of wonder and speculation. **Shilbottle, Snitter**? What of them? What do we make of a place that appears as **Schakelzerdesnoke** in 1264? What is **Prudhoe**? Why **Hexham**?

Apart from the sheer curiosity that these names arouse in us, the study of place-names is of great value to the historian. Chesters, streets and gates are still clues to Roman and pre-Roman forts and roads. **Gloster Hill** near Warkworth (in origin like the Gloucester in the South of England) might well be the site of a lost fortification – and a Roman altar stone was found there. Prehistoric burial mounds still persist in the Old English element *byrgen.* There is also the interest of coming across all those personal names that would never have reached us except through villages, farms and towns. And we have a picture of the swamps, the reeds, brightly-glittering streams, bare hills, wooded slopes, heavy clay land, pastures, beanfields, thorn bushes, farms where cheese was made or where bees were kept, fields of barley, of sheepfolds, pastures for calves, for deer and pigs, places where the heather grows. There were badgers, hares, wolves, foxes, otters, owls, hawks. There were the gallows where the felons were hanged. There was the holy-stone, the boundary marker, and there was the fortification. Altogether a varied, colourful canvas – a kind of Brueghel in names.

There are also later names that cannot find their way into a book such as this, because the study of place-names cannot take into account anything not deeply established. Yet GowkHill is the local dialect name for Cuckoo Hill, and Roughting Linn delightfully describes the noise of water at that ancient site: it bellows into its pond.

The book is arranged in such a way that all the common place-names elements are listed. Most are Old English, with strong affinities with other north European languages such as Old Norse; some are Middle English. Then follows a list of place-names in alphabetical order, based on the work of Dr. Allen Mawer and Professor Eilert Ekwall, whose scholarship is remarkable.

Elements used in Place-Names

The following list includes most of the elements, other than personal names, that occur in England. Examples are given of Northumberland names that contain these elements, and the examples demonstrate that it is not possible to guess from the modern spelling which elements are present: this information can only come from very early spellings.

The abbreviations used are O.E. (Old English) and M.E. (Middle English).

O.E. *ac* = oak
acen, aecen = of oaks. **Acton**
O.E. *aecer* = field, ploughed land. The Old Norse is *akr.* **Linacres**
O.E. *aeppel* = apple. **Apperley**
O.E. *aern* = house, especially storehouse.
O.E. *aesc* = ash tree, a very common place-name element in England. The Old Norse is askr.
aescen = of ash. **Ashington**
O.E. *aespe* = aspen.
O.E. *alor* = alder. **Allerwash**
O.E. *angr* = grassland. **Angerton, Ingram**
O.E. *baec* = back, and ridge (Old High German *bah*). **Backworth**
O.E. *baece,* bece = stream.
O.E. *baer* = pasture, especially for pigs.
M.E. *banke* = bank, ridge and hill (Old Danish *banke,* Old Norse *bakke*).
O.E. *bar* = boar.
O.E. *beag* = ring, circle.
O.E. *beam* = tree, beam. It can mean a footbridge made of a single beam.
O.E. *bean* = bean. This is fairly common. **Beanley**
O.E. *beg, beger* = berry. **Barmoor**
O.E. *beo* = bee. **Bewick**
O.E. *beonet* = reeds, rushes, coarse grasses.
O.E. *beorce* = birch. **Birkenside**
birce
O.E. *beorg* = hill, mound (especially a burial mound) Old Scandinavian *berg, biarg.* **Wooperton**
O.E. *beorht* = bright. **Birtwell**
O.E. *bere* = barley, and corn. **Berwick**
O.E. *berern* = barn.
O.E. *blaec* = black, dark-coloured (e.g., water, soil, the colour of a hill or forest). **Blakehope**
O.E. *boc* = beech. **Bockenfield**
O.E. *boga* = bow, such as the bend in a river.
O.E. *bolum* = tree trunks. **Bolam**
O.E. *botl, bold* = building. **Shilbottle**

O.E. *botn* = bottom, often in the sense of a valley or dell.
O.E. *brad* = broad, wide. **Bradford**
O.E. *braec* = brake, copse, thicket.
O.E. *braer, brer* = briar. **Barrow Law, Brierdene**
O.E. *bremel, braemel* = bramble.
O.E. *brerd* = rim, border, bank.
O.E. *bridd* = bird.
O.E. *broc* = marsh, brook, stream. Usually "brook" in the north. **Broxfield**
O.E. *brocc* = badger. **Brockley Hall**
O.E. *brom* = broom. **Broomley**
O.E. *brycg* = bridge. **Corbridge**
O.E. *bucc* = buck deer.
O.E. *bucca* = he-goat.
O.E. *bur* = cottage.
O.E. *burg, burh* = fortified place. **Burradon, Bamburgh**
O.E. *burna* (*burne*) = spring, brook, stream. "Burn" is commonly used in Northumberland for a small stream. **Brunton**
O.E. *by* = settlement (Old Norse *byr, boer*). **Byker**
O.E. *byge* = bend of a river. **Bywell**
Old West Saxon. *bygging* = building. **Newbiggin**
O.E. *byht* = bight, bend of a stream. **Nesbitt**
O.E. *byre* = shed, cattleshed.
O.E. *byrgen* = burial mound. **Hebron, Hepburn**
O.E. *caerse, cerse, cresse* = watercress. **Karswelleas**
O.E. *cald, ceald* = cold. **Catcherside**
O.E. *calf, cealf* = calf.
calfru, calfra = calves, of calves. } **Callaly, Callerton**
O.E. *calu* = bald, bâre.
O.E. *camp* = (from Latin *campus* – a field) an enclosed piece of land.
O.E. *carr* = rock. **Carham, Carraw**
O.E. *catt* = wild cat. It can also become a nickname. **Catton**
O.E. *ceaster, caester* = (from Latin "castra") a city or walled town, usually a Roman fort. It can apply to prehistoric fortifications, as we see in the "Chester Hill" type of name. It also appears as -caster, -castle, -cester. **Chesterhope**
O.E. *celde* = (from *ceald* = cold. M.E. *kelde* = spring). It can become "childe(e)". **Colwell**
O.E. *ceole* = throat in the sense of gorge, valley, neck of land. **?Chollerford**
O.E. *ceorl* = freeman. **Charlton**
O.E. *cese, cies* = cheese. **Cheswick**
M.E. *chace* = chase, hunting ground.
O.E. *cietel* = kettle, and a deep valley. **Chattlehope Burn**
O.E. *cild* = child. **Chirland**
O.E. *cinu* = chine, ravine.
O.E. *cipp* = beam, log. **Chipchase**
O.E. *cirice, cyrice* = church. **Chirdon**
O.E. *cis, cisen* = gravel, gravelly.
O.E. *claefre, clafre* = clover. **Clarewood**
O.E. *claeg* = clay.
O.E. *claene* = clean. **Clennell**
O.E. *clate, claete* = burdock.
O.E. *clif* = cliff, rock, steep drop, promontory, a slope, the bank of a river. **Heckley**
O.E. *cloh* = a ravine (dialect clough). **Catcleugh**
O.E. *clud* = rock.
O.E. *cnaepp* = hilltop, hillock.

O.E. *cnoll* = a knoll (small round hill).
O.E. *cocc* = cock, wild bird. **Coquet, Cocklaw**
O.E. *cofa* = cave, den. **?Coe Burn**
O.E. *col* = coal, charcoal. **?Cowden**
O.E. *copp* = hilltop. **Hawkhope**
O.E. *cot, cote* = cottage, shelter for animals (sheep). **Hepscott**
O.E. *cran* = crane. **?Cramlington**
O.E. *crawe* = crow. **Crawley**
O.E. *croft* = enclosed land for tillage or pasture. **Ancroft**
M.E. *crok* = crook, bend (Old Norse *krokr*). **Crookhouse**
O.E. *cros* = cross.
British. Old Welsh *cruc* = round hill or barrow mound (Irish *cruach*).
O.E. *crumb* = crooked. **Cronkley**
O.E. *cumb* = a coomb, deep hollow or valley.
O.E. *cweorn* = a mill, a quern. **Wharmley**
O.E. *cy* = cow. **Kyloe**
O.E. *cylen* = kiln. **Kilham**
O.E. *cyning* = king. **Kenton**
O.E. *dael* = valley. **Dalton**
O.E. *denn* = pasture.
O.E. *denu* = valley, dene. Very common in Northumberland. **Blagdon, Deanham**
O.E. *deop* = deep.
O.E. *deor* = deer. **Heatherslaw**
O.E. *dic* = ditch, moat, dike, embankment. Often describes a prehistoric rampart and ditch. **Detchant**
O.E. *docce* = dock, water-lily.
O.E. *duce* = duck.
O.E. *dun* = down, hill, and sometimes "hill pasture". **Dunstan**
O.E. *ea* = river (Old Scandinavian *a*) As a second element it usually occurs as -ey. **Ewart**
O.E. *ean* = lamb.
O.E. *ear* = gravel.
O.E. *earn* = eagle. **Yarnspath Law**
O.E. *ecg* = edge, a ridge, steep hill, hillside.
O.E. *edisc* = park, enclosed pasture.
O.E. *eg, ieg* = island, including a dry island in a marsh, land in a stream or between streams. It can be confused with *ea* (river). **Ponteland**
M.E. *ele* = a small island. It appears as -eels and eales.
O.E. *ellern* = elder tree. **Elford**
O.E. *eofor, efer* = wild boar.
O.E. *eowestre* = sheepfold.
Old Norse. *erg, aergi* = a shieling (hill pasture or hut on a pasture).
O.E. *ersc, aersc* = ploughed field, stubble field.
O.E. *erth, ierth, yrth* = ploughed land.
O.E. *faer* = passage. **?Lindisfarne**
O.E. *faesten* = stronghold.
O.E. *fag* = many-coloured. **Falstone, Fawdon**
O.E. *falod* = fold, pasture for deer.
O.E. *fealg, fealh, felh* } fallow, in the sense of ploughed land.
M.E. *falwe* } **Fallowlees**
O.E. *fealu* = fallow, pale brown colour, yellowish. **Fallowfield**
O.E. *fearn* = fern. **Fairnley**

O.E. *feld* = open country, plain – probably used in the sense of fields cleared from the old forests. It probably applies to an area larger than a "leah". **Felton**

O.E. *fen* = fen, marsh. **Fenton**
O.E. *fin* = a heap of wood. **Fenrother**
M.E. *flat* = a piece of level ground. **Flatworth**
O.E. *fleot* = creek, inlet, estuary. **Fleetham**
O.E. *flode* = a channel, stream. **?Flodden**
O.E. *fola* = foal. **Fowberry**
O.E. *ford* = ford. Very common. **Ford**
O.E. *foss* = a ditch.
O.E. *fugol* = wild bird.
O.E. *ful* = foul, dirty, rotten. **Philip**
O.E. *funta* = spring, and perhaps stream.
O.E. *fynig* = mouldy, marshy.
O.E. *fyrs* = furze.
O.E. *gaec* = cuckoo (dialect *gowk*).
O.E. *gaers* = grass (gaersen – grassy).
O.E. *galga* = gallows.
O.E. *gara* = a gore, a triangular piece of land, a strip of land. **Overgrass**

O.E. *gat*
Old Scandinavian. *geit* } = goat.

M.E. *garth* = yard, garden, paddock. In dialect *garth* can also mean a farm.

Old Norse, Old Swedish. *gata*
M.E. *gate* } = a road.

O.E. *gear* = weir, enclosure for catching fish.
O.E. *geard* = fence, hedge, enclosure. **Earle**
O.E. *geat, gaet* = a gate. Appears as yate and gate.
Old Norse *geil* = narrow ravine.
Old Norse *gil* = ravine, narrow valley.
O.E. *gos*(*a*) = goose. **Gosforth**
O.E. *graf* = grove, thicket.
O.E. *grene* = green, a grassy spot. **Grindon**
O.E. *greosn* = gravel, pebble.
O.E. *haecc* = hatch, gate, floodgate or sluice, a grating used to catch fish at a weir.
O.E. *haefen* = haven.

O.E. *haefer*
Old Norse. *hafr* } = he-goat.

O.E. (*ge*)*haeg* = hay, enclosed land, meadow. **Haining**
M.E. *hay* = forest fenced off for hunting.
O.E. *haes* = beech or oakwood, brushwood.
O.E. *haesel* = hazel (Old Scandinavian *hesli* = hazels).
O.E. *haeth* = heath plants, uncultivated land, heather. **Heddon**
O.E. *hafoc* = hawk. **Hawkhill**
O.E. *haga* = fence, fenced enclosure (Old Scandinavian *hagi*). It can appear as haugh, laugh, hough, law.
O.E. *haga* = hawthorn berry. **Hawden**
O.E. *halh, healh* = a corner, an angle, a secret place, recess, cave. In Northumberland it developed as "haugh", which is a piece of flat alluvial land by the side of a river. Originally this would have applied to land so formed by the bend of a river. **Beadnell, Bothal**
O.E. *halig* = holy. **Holystone**

O.E. *hals, heals* / Old Norse *hals* } = "neck", used in many senses. The Old Norse meaning is a projection, a narrow piece of land. The general sense is of a promontory, headland, projecting piece of land.

O.E. *ham* = village, estate, manor, homestead. One of the most common second elements. **Harnham**

O.E. *ham(m), hom(m)* = a meadow, especially by a stream, an enclosed plot of ground – probably its earliest meaning. It is difficult to distinguish this from *ham* above. **Fenham, Bellingham**

O.E. *hamel* / Old Norse *hamall* } = bare, treeless, from "maimed". **Humbleton Hill**

O.E. *han* = stone, rock.

O.E. *hana* = cock, wild bird.

O.E. *hangra* = a wood on the side of a steep hill. The old sense was "slope". **Hanging Leaves**

O.E. *har* = grey, hoary. **Harsondale**

Old Scandinavian (O.N.) *haugr* = heap, mound (especially a grave mound), hill. It is not always easy to distinguish it from O.E. *hoh.*

O.E. *heafod* = headland, summit, source of a stream, promontory. **Haltwhistle**

O.E. *heah* = high, tall. **Capheaton**

O.E. *hearg* = heathen place of worship, sacred grove. **?Kirkharle**

O.E. *heg, hieg, hig* = hay. **Aydon**

O.E. *hege* = hedge. **?Hazon**

O.E. *helde, hi(e)lde* = slope. **Learchild**

M.E. *helm* = "helmet", but used as a helmet-shaped cattle shed. **Helm**

O.E. *hengest* = stallion.

O.E. *henn* = hen. **Hinding Burn**

O.E. *heope* = rosehip. **Hepden Burn, Hepple**

O.E. *heorot* = hart, stag. **Hartburn**

O.E. *here* = army, host (Old Scandinavian *herr* = the whole people). **Harlow Hill**

O.E. *hid, higid* = hide, land enough to feed a family.

O.E. *hiwisc* = family, household.

O.E. *hlaw, hlaew* = hill, mound, burial mound (with a personal name). The form appears as -low, -loe, -law. Sometimes it is -ley. **Elilaw**

O.E. *hleo, hleow* = shelter, hut, refuge.

O.E. *hlid* = gate.

O.E. *hliep, hlyp, hlep* = leap, a place to be jumped over, steep drop. **Lipwood**

O.E. *hlinc* = lynchet, a bank separating strips of ploughed land on a slope. **Lynch Wood**

O.E. *hlose* = pig sty.

O.E. *hylnn* = a torrent, and a pool in M.E. (*linn*). **Lowlynn**

O.E. *hnecca* = a neck of land.

O.E. *hnoc* = wether sheep.

O.E. *hoc* = hook, bend.

O.E. *hoh* = heel, projecting ridge. In dialect this is hoe, heugh – a crag, cliff, precipice. In general its meaning varies from a slight rise to a steep ridge. **Cambo, Dunsheugh**

O.E. *holegn* = holly. **Hulne Park**

O.E. *hol(h)* = hollow, sunken, deep. **Holburn**

O.E. *hol(h)* = a hole, a deep place in water, a cave, a depression.

O.E. *holm* = small island, dry land in a fen. (Sometimes the spelling changes to -ham).

O.E. *hop* = dry land in a fen. Its usual meaning is the same as *hope* in dialect – a small enclosed valley, a branch valley, a blind valley. **Harehope**

O.E. *horn* = horn, corner, bend, tongue of land, horn-like projection. **Horncliffe**

O.E. *hraefn* = raven. **Ramshaw, Ravensheugh**
O.E. *hragra* = heron.
O.E. *hramsa* = wild garlic. **Ramshope**
O.E. *hreod* = reed. **Redburn**
Old Norse *hreysi, hreysar* = cairn.
O.E. *hring* = ring, circle.
O.E. *hris* = brushwood.
O.E. *hroc* = rook. **?Rochester**
Old Norse *hross* = horse.
O.E. *hrucge* = woodcock. **Rugley**
O.E. *hrung* = a pole.
O.E. *hrycg* = back, ridge (rigg). There are many "riggs".
M.E. *hule* = hut, hovel.
O.E. *hunig* = honey.
O.E. *hunta* = huntsman.
O.E. *hus* = house. **Newsham**
O.E. *hwaete* = wheat.

O.E. *hwamm* = literally "corner". A small valley or nook surrounded by high hills. **Whitwham**

O.E. *hweol* = wheel, circle.
O.E. *hwer* = kettle, cauldron.

O.E. *hwerfel, hwyrfel* = circle, whirlpool. It began as the fly-wheel of a spindle or a spiral. (Old Norse *hvirfill* means circle, crown of the head). **Whorlton**

O.E. *hwit* = white, light-coloured. **Witton, Whitley**
O.E. *hyll* = hill. **Ogle**

O.E. *hyrst*
M.E. *hurst* } Originally meaning "brushwood" it has come to mean wood, a sandy hill or knoll, a wooded hill. **Hirst**

-ing: In the "-ingas" form prefixed by a personal name it means the sons of-, the descendants of-, the tribe of-. The exact sense is not known, so in the place-names listed it has been given as "the people of".
Care has to be taken because "ing" can also be due to a change in another element (e.g., Ingram from Angerham). **Birling**

O.E. *iw* = yew.
Old Scandinavian *Karl* = freeman (O.E. *carl*).
Old Scandinavian *Kelda* = spring.
O.E. *lacu* = stream.
O.E. *lad, gelad* = road, path, water-course.

O.E. *laecc, lecc*
M.E. *lache, leche* } a stream flowing through boggy land. **Cawledge Park**

O.E. *laefer* = rush, yellow iris. **Learmouth**
O.E. *laege* = fallow.
O.E. *laes* = pasture.
O.E. *(ge)laetu* = junction (of roads, water).
O.E. *lam* = loam.
O.E. *lamb* = lamb. (O.E. plural *lambru*).

O.E. Old Norse *land* = land, estate, property, district. It is also used specifically in describing the quality of soil or type of tenure, whether it is cultivated, and what grows there. **Coupland**

O.E. *lang* = long. **Langley**

M.E. *launde* = glade, pasture, lawn. It is not easy to distinguish from *land* above.

O.E. *leah* = originally an open place in a wood, a glade, it has taken on a meaning of open land that is used as arable, and another main sense as "wood, forest".
Common forms are -ley, -leigh, lea, lee, with plurals lees, leese, leam. **Bradley, Cheveley**

O.E. *leoht* = light, bright, light-coloured. **Leighton Green**

O.E. *lin* = flax. **Linacres**

O.E. *lind* = limetree. **Linsheeles**

O.E. *lund* = grove, copse.

O.E. *maed* = meadow.

O.E. *mael* = mark, cross. **Meldon**

O.E. *(ge)maere* = boundary. Difficult to distinguish from "mere" (lake). **Greymare Hill**

O.E. *mearc* = boundary, boundary mark, border.

O.E. *meoluc* = milk (usually showing good pasture). **Melkridge**

O.E. *mere* = mere, lake. **Boulmer**

O.E. *mersc, merisc* = marsh. **Owmers**

O.E. *mid*
O.E. *middel* } = middle. A settlement between two others. **Middleton**

O.E. *micel* = large. **Mickley**

O.E. *mor* = moor, waste upland, fen. **Morwick**

O.E. *(ge)mot* = meeting place – of streams or people (moot).

O.E. *mutha* = river mouth. **Alnmouth**

O.E. *mylen* = mill. **Melkington, Milbourne**

Old Norse *myrr* = mire, bog.

O.E. *naeddre* = adder.

O.E. *naess* = headland, cape, ridge. **Fawns**

O.E. *neotherra* = lower. **Netherton**

O.E. *netele* = nettle.

O.E. *ofer* = river bank, border, margin, sometimes a steep slope or a ridge. **Wooler**

O.E. *ora* = border, margin (very much like *ofer*).

O.E. *paeth* = path. This is still commonly used. **Morpeth**

O.E. *pen(penn)* = enclosure, pen.

O.E. *peru* = pear (*pirige, pyrige* = pear-tree).

O.E. *pisu, piosu, peosu* = pea.

O.E. *plume* = plum, plum-tree.

O.E. *pol* = pool, deep place in a river, tidal stream. The Welsh "*poll*" is the source of Pow, a slow-moving stream.

O.E. *port:* from Latin "portus" = harbour, town. **Portgate**
from Latin "porta" = gate.

O.E. *pyll* = tidal creek, stream.

M.E. *quarrere* = quarry. **?Whirleyshaws**

O.E. *ra* = roe-deer. **Raylees**

O.E. *racu* = in a compound *ea-*, stream – *racu*, meaning the bed of a stream or water course.

O.E. *rad* = riding, and road.

O.E. *raew, raw* = row (of houses) hedgerow. **Catraw**

O.E. *ramm* = ram.

O.E. *read* = red. **Rede River**
O.E. *ric* = stream, ditch.
O.E. *rima* = rim, border, bank, coast. **Rimside Moor**
O.E. *risc, rysc* = rush.
O.E. *rith, rithe, rithig* = a small stream. (Old Low German ritha, rithe). **Ritton**
O.E. *rocc* = rock. **Rock**
O.E. *rod* = rood, cross. **Rodestane**
O.E. *roth, rothu* = clearing. **Roddam**
O.E. *ruh* = rough, uncultivated ground. **Rowhope**
O.E. *ryding* = clearing, cleared land. **Riding**
O.E. *ryge* = rye. **Ryal**
O.E. *sae* = lake, sea. **Monkseaton**
O.E. *saeppe* = spruce fir.
O.E. *saet* = trap.
O.E. *saete* = seat. **Simonside**
Old Norse. *saetr* = a shieling, hill pasture.
O.E. *salh, sealh* = sallow (plant). } **Saltwick**
O.E. *salt, sealt* = salt (*saltere* = salt-worker, salt-seller) } **Saltwick**
O.E. *sand* = sand. **Sandhoe**
O.E. *scaga* = shaw, thicket, grove. **Elishaw**
O.E. *scald, sceald* = shallow. **Shadfen, Shawdon**
O.E. *scead* = boundary.
O.E. *sceaft* = shaft, pole. **Shaftoe**
O.E. *sceap, scep, scip* = sheep. **Shipley**
O.E. *sceard* = notch, gap.
O.E. *scearn* = dung, mud.
O.E. *scearp* = sharp, rugged, steep. **Sharperton**
O.E. *scearu* = boundary.
O.E. *sceat* = a strip of land, usually overgrown, or even a park. **Bebside**
O.E. *scene, sciene* ≙ beautiful, bright.
M.E. *schele* = (dialect sheel, shiel) hut, shed. **Agarshill, North Shields**
O.E. *scipen* = shippon, byre, cattle-shed.
O.E. *scir* = clear, bright.
O.E. *scora* = shore in the sense of steep rock, bank, hill. **Shoresworth**
O.E. *scraef* = cave, den, hovel, hollow, ravine.
O.E. *screawa* = shrewmouse. } **Scrainwood**
M.E. *schrewe* = shrew, but also rascal, villain } **Scrainwood**
O.E. *scylf, scelf* = rock, crag, ledge. **Shilvington**
O.E. *scyttel, scyttels* = bar, bolt, arrow. **Chesters (Scytlescester)**
O.E. *setl* = seat, dwelling place.
O.E. *sid* = broad, spacious.
O.E. *side* = side, a hillside (M.E. *side* = slope of a hill, especially a long one).
Old Norse *sker* = rock, reef (English *"scar"* – rock, crag).
Old Norse *skogr* } = wood.
M.E. *scogh* } = wood.
O.E. *slaed* = valley, dell. **Weedslade**
O.E. *slaep* = a slippery, miry place.
M.E. *slag* = slippery with mud, muddy. **Slaggyford**
O.E. *smeoru* = butter.
O.E. *smethe* = smooth.
O.E. *snaed, snad* = land, clearing.
O.E. *sol* = muddy place, wallowing place for animals.
O.E. *spic* = bacon. There is, however, another similar word with quite a different meaning. Dutch *"spik"* is a bridge made of treetrunks or brushwood. Low German has *"spike"* – a brushwood causeway. **Wansbeck River**

O.E. *spring, spryng* = spring, well. But M.E. *"spring"* also means a plantation.
O.E. *staener* = stony ground.
O.E. *staeth* = landing-place.
O.E. *stall, steall* = place, stable, stall. **Whittonstall**
O.E. *stan* = stone, stones. This can refer to special stones, such as monoliths, Roman mileposts, paved roads (Roman), unusual stones that are renowned for their shape, size or position, stones used for meeting places, etc. (Old Norse *"steinn"* = stone). **Featherstone, Stannington**
O.E. *stapol* = post, pillar.
O.E. *steap* = steep.
O.E. *stede, styde* = site, "Stede" is often used to refer to farms, especially dairy farms. **Newstead**
O.E. *stig* = path. **Styford**
O.E. *stig* = pigsty.
O.E. *stigol* = stile, steep ascent. The word *"steel"* came from this, and means a ridge, precipice, steep path up a ridge.
O.E. *stoc* = monastery, cell, or just place – especially a place dependent on another. **Stocksfield**
O.E. *straet, stret* = street, Roman road, or other paved road.
O.E. *strand* = shore.
O.E. *strod* = marshy land overgrown with brushwood. **Broadstruthers Burn**
M.E. *strother* = marsh, swamp. **Coldstrother**
O.E. *styrc, styric, steorc* = young bullock or heifer.
O.E. *sulh* = a plough.
O.E. *suth* = south. **North Sunderland**
O.E. *swaer, swar* = heavy. **Swarland**
O.E. *swin* = swine, wild boar. **Swinhoe**
O.E. *teag* = enclosure.
O.E. *thing* = meeting place, court (Old Scandinavian – assembly, parliament). It appears as ting-, fing-, thing-. **Dingbell Hill**
O.E. *thorn* = thorn bush. **Thorngrafton**
O.E. *thorp, throp* = farm, hamlet. Probably *"throp"* was a dependent farm. *"Thorp"* is especially common in Denmark and Sweden, and in England "thorpes" are common in Danish settlements. **Throphill**
O.E. *thyrel* = perforated, having a hole. **Thirlwall**
O.E. *thyrne* = thorn bush (Old Scandinavian *"thyrnir"*). **Farnham, Caistron**
O.E. *thyrre* = dry.
O.E. *thyrs* = giant, demon.
O.E. *ticcen* = kid.
M.E. *tod* = fox. **Tod Hill**
Old Scandinavian *toft, topt* = site of a house, a deserted site, a homestead.
O.E. *torr* = high rock, peak, hill (Gaelic *torr*).
O.E. *tot* = look-out. **Tosson**
O.E. *totaern* = watch-tower.
O.E. *treo(w)* = tree, usually a prominent or unusual one. **Trewick**
O.E. *trog* = a trough, then hollow or valley shaped like a trough. **Trows**
O.E. *tun* = originally a fence or enclosure, but it soon became a homestead, village or town. On the whole names ending in -tun tend to be later than *-ham.*
Its most general meaning is homestead or village, but it can also mean an outlying farm. **Alwinton**

O.E. *twisla* = fork of a river, land in the fork of a river. **Twizel**
O.E. *uferra* = upper.
O.E. *ule* = owl. **Ulgham, Outchester**
Old Scandinavian *ulfr* = wolf (O.E. *wulf*). **Wooden**
O.E. *unthances* = without leave (it becomes *unthank*) – a squatter's land. **Unthank**
O.E. *ut, uterra* = out, outer.
Old Norse *veggr* = wall.
Old Scandinavian *vithr* = wood.
Old Scandinavian *vik* = bay.
Old Scandinavian *vra* = corner, nook, remote place.
O.E. *(ge) waed* = ford.
O.E. *waegn* = wain, wagon. **Wansbeck**
O.E. *wael* = a well, a deep pool, deep water in a stream.
O.E. *(ge) waesc* = wash. **Sheepwash**
O.E. *waesse* = wet place, swamp. **Allerwash**
O.E. *waet, wet* = wet. **Weetwood**
O.E. *wald, weald* = wood, high forest land, then open upland, waste ground.
O.E. *walh, wealh* = Briton (plural *walas, wealas*) – also serf.
O.E. *wall, weall* = wall, especially referring to prehistoric and Roman forts, and to Hadrian's Wall. **Wallsend**
O.E. *weard* = watch. **Warden**
O.E. *wearg* = outlaw, criminal, felon, and the place where they were executed. **Wreighill**
O.E. *weg* = way, road. **Stannington**
O.E. *welig, wilig* = willow.
O.E. *well, wiell, waell* = well, spring, stream. **Weldon**
O.E. *weoh* = holy place, heathen temple. **Wooperton**
O.E. *(ge) weorc* = work, fortification. **Wark**
O.E. *wer* = wier, dam. **Flotterton**
O.E. *wic* = (Latin *vicus*) dwelling, dwelling-place, village, hamlet, town, farm. Probably the most common meaning is dairy-farm. **Alnwick**
O.E. *wice* = wych elm.
O.E. *wiht* = bend, curve.
O.E. *wilde* = waste, uncultivated land.
O.E. *winn* = meadow, pasture. **Heddon (East and West)**
O.E. *wisc* = damp meadow, marsh.
O.E. *withig* = willow (there is a side-form O.E. *widig* -widdy – a withy). **Weedslade**
O.E. *worth* = originally a fence or enclosure, then homestead. It continued for a long time in forming place-names. **Warkworth**
O.E. *wrecca* = outlaw. **Ratchwood**
O.E. *wrid, writh, gewrid* = bush, thicket.
O.E. *wudu* = wood, forest, timber. **Coquet**
O.E. *wyrm* = reptile, worm, serpent.
O.E. *wyrt* = plant, vegetable.

An Alphabetical List of Place-Names of Northumberland

---

1. The places are arranged alphabetically. Almost all of them appear on the 1 inch to the mile Ordnance Survey maps. Very few do not appear on any modern map – they are indicated by an asterisk.

2. The grid with its numbered squares covers the whole county. Each large square corresponds on the 1 inch map to 100 kilometre squares at 10 square intervals, so it is easy to look for places on the 1 inch map. Brackets around a number refer to a wide location – a river or stream.

3. The earliest spelling is given and its date.

4. The possible elements of the name are given and the meaning.

5. Sometimes there is a difference between Allen Mawer and Professor Ekwall in analysis, and many of the names in Mawer's book do not appear in Ekwall's. Where I wish to show some of these differences I have used the abbreviations Ek (Ekwall) and M (Mawer).

6. As it is impossible to be precise in interpreting such elements as -ham, -wic and -tun, one must assume that farm, settlement, etc., are interchangeable in many cases. It stands to reason that any settlement was based on agriculture anyway.

14	Abberwick	Alburwic 1170	The *wic* (dwelling) of Alu(h)burg (a woman).
12	Abshiels	Abscheles 1286	(O.E) Abba's house
5	Acklington	Eclinton 1177	The *tun* (settlement) of Eadlac's people (Ek) or Aeccel (M)
29	Acomb	Akum 1268	O.E. *acum* = at the oaks.
28	Acton	Akedene 1269	O.E. *ac-denu* = oak valley.
13	Acton	Aketon 1242	O.E. *ac-tun* = oak farm or Aca's *tun* (Ek).
16	Adderstone	Edredeston 1233	Eadred's *tun* (settlement).
48	Agars Hill	Algerseles 1278	Ealdgar's house (M).
35	Akeld (ay-keld)	Achelda 1169	O.E. *ac-helde* = oak slope. (M thinks that it could mean *a* + *kelda* – a river and well or spring – forming a marshy place on the edge of the Till valley.)
***32**	Akenside	Akenside 1332	The side of a hill covered with oaks.

11	Aldworth	Aldewurth 1120	Ealda's *worth* (homestead) or old worth.
(38)	Allen River	Alwent 1275	Like the River Alwin.
(38)	Allendale	Alwentedal 1226	Alwin valley.
38	Allendale town	Aleweton 1245	(Settlement) on the river.
37	Allerdean	Elredene 1108	Aelfhere's valley (M).
34	Allerhope Burn	Alrehopeburn 1240	Alder valley.
39	Allerwash	Alrewes 1202	O.E. *Alra* (aller)–*waesse* Alder swamp.
(26)	Allery Burn	Alriburn 1292	O.E. *Alra-burn*=burn of the alders.
(14)	Aln	Alaunos 150, Alne 730	A British (pre-Roman) river name.
34	Alnham	Alneham 1228	(O.E.) Settlement on the Aln.
6	Alnmouth	Anyemue 1205, Alnemuth 1230 (which Ekwall records as 1201)	(O.E.) Mouth of the Aln.
14	Alnwick (annik)	Alauna 150, Alnewick 1160 (M), Alnewich 1178 (Ek)	Homestead or farm on the river Aln.
(33)	Alwin R.	Alewent 1200	A British river name.
33	Alwinton	Alwenton 1242	O.E. *tun* on the river. River settlement.
5	Amble	Ambell 1204	Anna's promontory.
6	Amerston	Aymundeston 1243	Eymundr's farm (M).
27	Ancroft	Ancroft 1180 (M) Anecroft 1195 (Ek)	O.E. *an* – one, *ana* – lonely. Lonely croft.
21	Angerton	Angerton 1186	O.E. *angr–tun* (settlement on the grassland).
29	Anick	Aeilnewic 1160	Egelwin's (Ek) or Aethelwine's (M) *wic* (farm).
18	Apperley	Appeltreleg 1201	(O.E.) Apple-tree clearing
28	Ardley	Herdeley 1228	(O.E.) Earda's clearing (M).
3	Ashington	Essende 1170, Essenden 1205	O.E. *aescen-denu* = a valley overgrown with ash trees (M. says that it is O.E. Aescinga – *denu*: valley of Aesc or of his sons).
19	Aydon	Ayden 1225, 1242	O.E. *heg-denn*=hay pasture.
14	Aydon	Aydun 1279	O.E. *heg-dun*=hay hill.
28	Aydon Shiels	Aldenscheles 1341	Ealdwine's house (M).
58	Ayle Burn River	Alne 1347	Aln.
2	Backworth	Bachisurda, Bacwrth 1271	(O.E.) Bacca's *worth.* (homestead).
42	Bagraw	Bagraw 1385	O.E. *raw* = a row (of houses) M.E. *bagger-badger* = a hawker (M. gives this as Bacga's row).
16	Bamburgh	Bebbanburh 547	(O.E.) Bebba's fort. Bebba was, according to Bede, Aethelfrith's queen.
48	Barhaugh	Berhalu 1279	O.E. *bere-healh*: barley haugh.
18	Barley Hill	Birlawe 1225	O.E. *bere-hlaw*: barley hill.
26	Barmoor	Beiremor 1231	O.E. *beger* = berries. Cranberry moor (but M. gives this as Beaghere's *mor*).
30	Barrasford	Barwisford 1242	O.E. *bearu, bearwes* = by a grove. Ford by a grove.
33	Barrow Law	Brerylawe 1304	M.E. *brere* = briar. O.E. *hlaw* = hill.

24	Barton	Barton 1199	O.E. *bara-tun* = bare farm, *bar-tun* = boar enclosure; *bere-tun* = barley farm. The change of sound from e to a did not take place in the 12th century, so the last meaning is less possible than the others (M).
31	Bavington	Parva Babington 1242	The settlement of Babba's people.
7	Beadnell	Bedehal 1161	(O.E.) Beda's – *halh* (Ek). Bedwine's *healh* (M). The *halh* in Northumberland is usually the same as "haugh".
27	Beal	Behil 1208 (Ek), Beyl 1228	O.E. *beo-hyll* = bee hill. Probably this was where the bees liked to swarm.
24	Beanley	Benelega(m) 1150	O.E. *bean-leah* = beanfield or clearing.
29	Beaufront	Beaufroun 1356	Beautiful brow (its position faces south across the Tyne valley).
30	Beaumont	Beaumont 1232	French: fine hill.
3	Bebside	Bibeshet 1198	(O.E.) Bibba's *sceat* or *(ge)set*= Bibba's piece of land or dwelling.
3	Bedlington	Bedlington 1050	The *tun* (farm, settlement) of Bedla's or Betla's people.
10	Bellasis	Beleassis 1279	Old French *assise*= beautiful site.
16	Belford	Beleford 1242	It looks like Bella's ford, but this personal name does not appear anywhere else. It could be O.E. *bel-haga* = a glade in a forest, or dry land in a swamp.
41	Bellingham (inj)	Bainlingham 1170	Ek says that this is the *ham* of the hill-dwellers. M. takes it to be the homestead of Beola's or Bella's people.
49	Bellister	Belester 1279	Old French *bel-estre*, meaning a fine place (Ek). M. sees it as Bella's *ceaster*, or fortified place. (There is clearly in Ek. an unwillingness to accept M.'s "Bella" as a personal name.)
43	Bell Shiel	Belleshope 1330	(O.E.) Bell's valley (M).
10	Belsay	Bilesho 1163	Bill's-*hoh*, or ridge (Ek. sees "Bill" as a short form of Bilfrith, Bilheard, etc.)
11	Benridge	Benerig 1242	O.E. *bean-hrycg* = a ridge where the beans grew.
1	Benton, Little- Long-	Bentune 1190 Parva Bentona 1236 Magna Beneton 1256	O.E. *beonet-tun* or *bean-tun* = Farm on the coarse grass, or bean farm.
1	Benwell	Bynnewalle 1050	O.E. *bionnan-walle* = the place inside the (Roman) wall.
27	Berrington	Berigdon 1208 Beringdon 1269	Most likely to be O.E. *byrigdun* a hill with a fort on it. M. suggests the hill of Bere's people.

10	Berwick Hill	Berewic 1205 Berewic Super Montem 1428	O.E. *bere-wic*: barley farm.
27	Berwick-upon-Tweed	Berewich 1167	Barley farm.
25	Bewick	Beuuiche 1136 Bowich 1167	O.E. *beo-wic* = bee-farm.
33	Bickerton	Bikertun 1236	O.E. *beocere-tun* = bee-keeper's settlement or farm.
33	Biddlestone	Bitnesden 1181 (Ek) Bitlesden 1181 (M)	O.E. *bytle* (or *botl*)*-denu* = a dwelling in a valley, or the valley of Bidel, Bydel or Bitel (M).
1	Billy Mill	Molendinum de Billing 1320	(O.E.) Billing's mill (M).
6	Bilton	Bylton 1242	Bil(l)a's *tun.*
30	Bingfield	Bingefeld 1181	The *feld* (field) of Bynna's people.
15	Birchope	Byrchensop 1325	Possibly Beorhtwine's *hop* (M.) or birch-*hop* (valley).
18	Birkenside	Byrkinside 1262	Birch slope.
5	Birling	Berlinga 1187	Baerla's people.
20	Bitchfield	Bechefeud 1242	O.E. *bece-feld* = beechfield.
52	Black Blakehope	Blachope 1230	O.E. *blaec-hop* = black valley.
***16**	Blackmiddingmore	Blacmyddingmore 1333	The M.E. *middying* means a dung-heap, so this moor must have been a foul place.
13	Black Lough	Blakemere 1200	Black mere.
2	Blagdon	Blakedenn 1203	O.E. *blaec-denu* = black valley.
25	Blakelaw	Blakelawe 1251	Black hill.
28	Blanchland	Blanchelande 1165	French = white glade (a name transferred from Normandy).
59	Blenkinsopp	Blencheneshopa 1178	(Blenkin's) valley, or Welsh *blaen* = top valley.
(3)	Blyth River (bleye)	Blitha 1204 Blye 1257	O.E. *blithe* means gentle, merry, but the origin of this name may be pre-Roman (M).
3	Blyth	Blida 1130 Snoc de Bliemue 1208 Blithmuth 1236	The town site is referred to as the mouth of the River Blyth and a "snook" or projection of land.
12	Bockenfield	Bokenfeld 1206	O.E. *bocen-feld* = a beechfield.
21	Bolam	Bolum 1155	O.E. *bol-ham* = a settlement on a rounded hill, or O.E. *bolum* = the tree trunks (Ek).
14	Bolton	Bolton 1200	O.E. *botl-tun* = a place with a building on it, or a village.
3	Bothal (botl)	Bothalle 1233 Bothala 1271	(O.E.) Bota's *halh* (i.e., land by the river).
6	Boulmer (oom)	Bulemer 1161	O.E. *bulan-mere* = bullock's or bull's mere (in this case the shallow rock pools).
46	Bowmont Water	Bolbenda 1050	(The meaning is not clear, but it does refer literally to a bend in the river.)
37	Bowsden	Bolesdon 1195 Bollesdene 1228	Either O.E. *botl-dun* (a hill dwelling) (Ek); or Boll's valley or hill (M).

	Bradford	Bradeford 1212	Same meaning: a broad ford.
16	(1) near Bamburgh		
20	(2) near Bolam	Bradeford 1242	
49	Bradley	Bradeley 1279	O.E. *brad-leah* = broad clearing (M).
5	Brainshaugh	Bregesne 1104	From a side-form of "borrans" – a burial mound (Ek) or Bregwine's haugh (M).
24	Brandon	Bremdona 1150 Bromdun 1236	O.E. *brom-dun* and *bremen-dun,* a broom hill, or broomy hill.
14	Branton	Bremetona 1150	O.E. *bremen-tun* = a farm where the broom grew.
46	Branxton	Brankeston 1195	Branoc's *tun* (settlement).
(24)	Breamish River	Bromic 1050	A pre-Roman river name, perhaps like the Welsh *brefu* – to roar.
2	Brenkley	Brinchelawa 1178	Brynca's *hlaw* (hill or mound).
4	Brierdene	Brerden 1295	(O.E.) briar valley.
12	Brinkburn	Brinkeburne 1188	Brynca's burn, but O.E. *brinc(e)* also means the brink of a hill, a steep slope.
35	Broadstruthers Burn (Cheviot)	Bradstoir 1255	O.E. *brad-strod* = broad strother (marshy ground overgrown with brushwood).
15	Brockley Hall	Brockleygehirst 1309	O.E. *brocc-hyrst* = badger wood.
19	Broomhaugh	Brunhalwe 1242 (Ek)	A broom-covered haugh.
18	Broomley	Bromley 1242 (Ek)	O.E. *brom-leah,* a broom groove.
5	Brotherwick	Brotherwyc 1242	Brodor's *wic* (farm).
25	Brownridge	Brunrige 1330	(O.E.) brown ridge.
7	Broxfield	Brokesfeud 1256	Field on the brook (Ek) or Badger's field (M).
7	Brunton	Burneton Batayll 1242	O.E. *burna-tun* = settlement by the burn.
1	Brunton (E,W,N,S)	Burneton 1242	O.E. *burna-tun* = brook farm.
26	Buckton	Buketon 1208	(O.E.) Bucca's farm.
16	Budle	Bolda 1166, Bodle 1197	O.E. *botl* = dwelling.
28	Bulbeck Common	Bolebec 1236	Named after the Norman French village Bolbec, at the mouth of the Seine.
2	Burradon (rdn)	Burgdon 1242	O.E. *burg-dun* = hill with a fort.
33	Burradon	Burwedon 1242	O.E. *burg-dun* = a hill with a fortification on it.
16	Burton	Burton 1242	O.E. *burh-tun* = a fortified settlement.
5	Buston, High-, Low-	Buttesdune 1166 (Ek)	O.E. Buteles-*dun* – possibly Butel's hill.
41	Buteland	Boteland 1242	Bota's land.
9	Butter Law	Buterlawe 1242	Butter hill.
1	Byker	Bilkere 1196	Old Scandinavian *by-kiarr* – which means the village marsh.
19	Bywell-on-Tyne	Biguell 1104	O.E. *byge-wella* = spring at the bend (of the river).
33	Caistron	Cers 1160 Kersten 1184 (M)	M.E. *Kers* – O.E. *thyrne* = thorn bush by the carse (marsh).
23	Callaly	Calualea 1161	O.E. *calfa-leah* = pasture for calves.

10	Callerton	Caluerduna 1100	O.E. *calfra-dun* = hill where the calves grazed.
9	Black Callerton	Calverdona 1212	
10	High Callerton	Calverdon 1242	
21	Cambo	Camho 1230	O.E. *camb-hoh* = spur of a hill with a crest.
3	Cambois (Kamus)	Cammes 1050 Cambus 1204	Welsh *cemmaes,* Irish *camus* – a bay – from Old Celtic *kambo,* meaning crooked. Cambois stands on a curving bay.
21	Capheaton	Magna Heton 1242 Cappitheton 1454	O.E. *hea-tun* = a settlement on high land. Latin *caput* = chief. Chief village on high land.
46	Carham-on-Tweed	Carrum 1050	O.E. *carrum* = at the rocks (Ek) or O.E. *carr-ham* = homestead by the rock.
40	Carraw	Charrau 1279	O.E. *carr-raw* = a rocky ridge.
51	Carriteth	le Caryte 1325	Old Norman French *carite(dh)* = land used for a charitable or religious purpose.
23	Cartington	Cretenden 1220	Cretta-*dun* = the hill of Certa's people (Ek). (M. thinks that it is Kiartan's hill – a Scandinavian name).
30	Carrycoats	Carricot 1245	It might be Celtic *caer-y-coed* = fort in the wood (M).
3	Catchburn	Cacheborn 1279	O.E. Caecca's stream (?)
31	Catcherside	Calcherside 1270	M.E. *Caldchere-side* = cold-cheer hill.
53	Catcleugh Shin	Cattechlow 1279	O.E. *catte-cloh* = the "clough" or ravine of the wild cats. "Shin" is Scottish for a steep hill slope. (M. thinks it could also be a personal name, Catta).
2	Catraw	Catrawe 1479	O.E. *raw* = cat's row or Catta's row.
38	Catton	Catteden 1229	Wild-cat valley.
12	Causey Park	La Chauce 1242	M.E. *cauce, cause* from Old Norman French *cauciee,* French *chausee* = a paved way. The Devil's Causey (Causeway) is the Roman road.
6	Cawledge Park	Caweleg 1241 Cauleche 1252	M.E. *leche, lache* means a long narrow swamp through which the water course moves slowly. It is possible that *"cau"* could be jackdaw or crow.
41	Charlton	Carlton 1195	O.E. *ceorla-tun* = freeman's farm.
15	Charlton -North, -South	Charleton del North, Suth 1242	O.E. *ceorla-tun* = freeman's farm.
53	Chattlehope Burn	Chetilhopp 1320	O.E. *cietel-hop* = kettle-shaped hop (blind valley).
25	Chatton	Chetton 1178	O.E. *Ceatta-tun* = Ceatta's farm.
20	Cheeseburn Grange	Cheseburgh 1286	O.E. A burg is a fortification, so the association of this with cheese is unusual.
31	Chesterhope	Chestrehop 1298	O.E. *hop* (valley) by the fort.

30	Chesters	Scytlescester 1104	O.E. Scytles-*ceaster,* which is either Scyttel's fort or O.E. *scyttles,* which means bar or bolt. Perhaps the old fort could have been used as an enclosure for animals.
27	Cheswick (Chizik)	Chesewic 1208	O.E. *ciese-wic* = cheese farm.
4	Cheveley	Chiveleye 1300	Ceofa's or Cifa's *leah* (glade, clearing, meadow).
4	Chevington	Cebbingtun 1050 Chiuingtona 1212	Ceofa's or Cifa's peoples' settlement.
35	Cheviot (Chev or Chiv)	Chiuiet 1182	This is a pre-Roman name, and its meaning is unknown.
4	Chibburn	Chibrnemue 1228 Chilburne 1292	This might be Cilla's stream.
25	Chillingham	Cheulingeham 1187	The settlement of Ceofel's people. Ceofel is derived from the name that we see in Cheveley and Chevington – Ceofa.
40	Chipchase	Chipches 1229	O.E. *cipp-ceas* = a log structure (such as an animal trap (Ek). M. gives this as Chip's chase – but this seems less likely. (O.E. Cippa – a personal name.)
51	Chirdon	Chirden 1255	O.E. *cyric* = church. This could mean either a valley with a church in it or a valley with a bend. (O.E. *cierr.*) Chirdon is on a winding stream.
1	Chirton	Cheriton 1203	O.E. *Cyrictun* = church-tun, a piece of land or settlement belonging to a church, or with a church on it. (M. thinks that the first element may be a personal name Ceorra.)
23	Chirland (Chirnells Moor)	Childerlund 1178	O.E. *cildra-land* (*cild* = child). This could refer to land that belongs to a young noble awaiting Knighthood (e.g., as in Childe Harold, Wynd, Roland).
30	Chollerford and Chollerton	Only Chollerton (Choluerton 1175) is listed.	The ford was probably named first and could mean either that it belonged to Ceola, or that it was a ford in a *ceol* (gorge). Chollerton would then be the homestead by Ceolan ford (Ceola's ford) or Ceolford.
3	Choppington	Cebbington 1050	O.E. *Ceabbing(a)tun* = Ceabba's people's settlement.
19	Clarewood	Claverworth, Clareworth 1212	O.E. *claefre-worth* = clover enclosure.
33	Clennell	Clenil 1181	Literally a "clean hill", which means that it would have been free of weeds or hurtful growth.
3	Clifton	Clifton 1242	Farm on a hill or slope.
58	Coanwood	Collanwode 1279	(O.E.) Collan's wood.

NORTHUMBERLAND

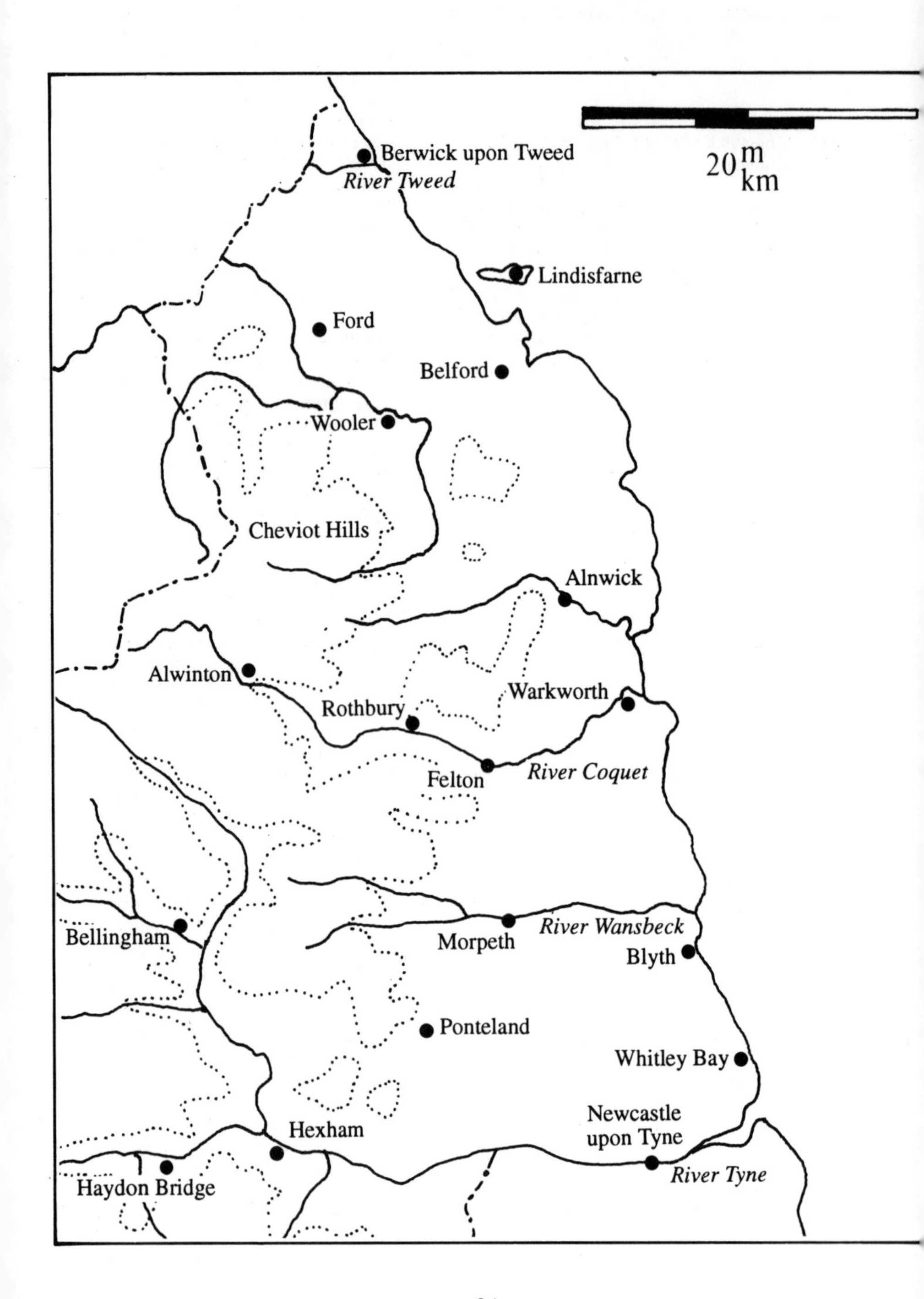

NORTHUMBERLAND *divided into squares to show location of place-names* (See page 17).

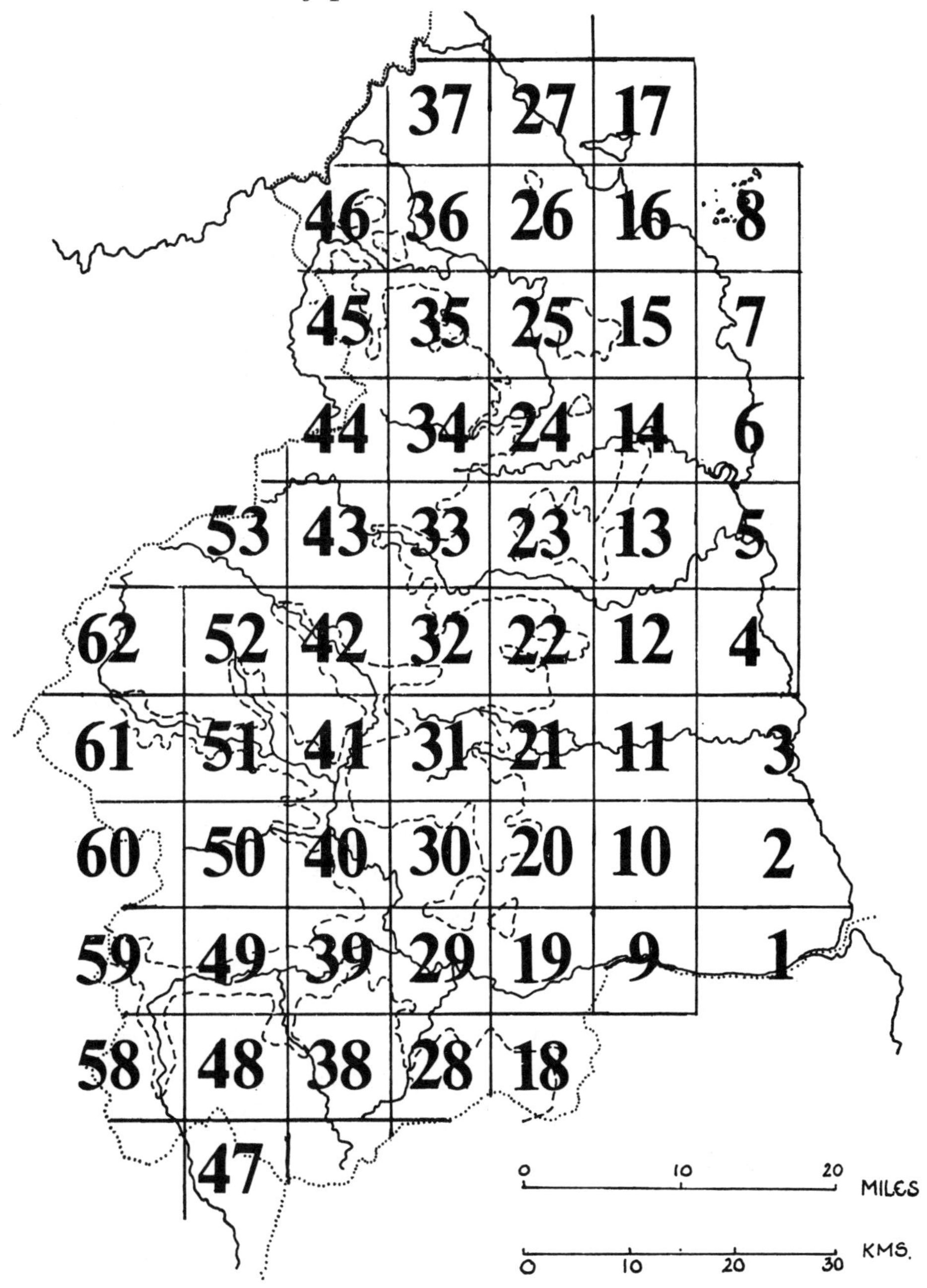

29	Coastley	Cotisley 1250	(O.E.) Cocc's clearing (M).
15	Cocklaw	Creklawe 1296	O.E. *cocc-hlaw* = wild bird hill.
4	Cockle Park	Cockhill 1314	O.E. *cocc-hyll* = wild bird hill.
23	Coe Burn	Coveburn 1295	This probably refers to the rock overhangs and small caves in the rocks near where the stream flows.
10	Coldcoats	Caldecotes 1242	Cold cots (cottage or sheep shelter).
(33)	Coldlaw Burn	Caldelauburne 1255	O.E. Cold stream.
25	Coldmartin	Calemerton 1195	O.E. *mere-tun* = farm by the cold mere or pool.
20	Coldstrother	Caldestrother 1232	O.E. Cold, marshy ground overgrown with brushwood.
21	Coldwell	Colewell 1277	O.E. Cool stream or spring.
30	Coldwell	Caldewell 1325	O.E. Cool stream or spring.
3	Coldwell	Caldewell 1242	O.E. Cool stream or spring.
28	Colpits	Colpittes 1255	Coal pits.
30	Colwell	Colewell 1236	O.E. *cole-wielle* = cool spring or O.E. *col-wielle* = coal spring.
(13)	Coquet River (Coek't)	Cocwud(a) 1050 Coqued 1104	(O.E.) *cocwudu* is a forest where cocks or wild birds live.
5	Coquet Island	Insula Coket 1135	
(23)	Coquetdale	Cokedale 1160	The valley of the river Coquet.
29	Corbridge	Corebricg 1050	This name, literally Corbridge, came from the Roman site Corstopitum at Corchester, so Cor- is a shortened form of the old Roman name, the meaning of which is not clear.
46	Cornhill-on-Tweed	Cornehale 1208	O.E. Cranes' *halh* (haugh).
31	Corsenside	Crossinset 1254	Probably the Irish personal name Crossan – Old Norse *saetr*, a shieling or hill pasture. Crossan's hill pasture.
11	Cottingwood	Cotingwud 1257	O.E. Cotta's people's wood (M).
53	Cottonshope	Cotteneshopp 1230	O.E. Probably Cot(t)en's or Cot(t)a's valley or field.
36	Coupland	Coupland 1242	Old Norse. *Kaupland* = bought land.
30	Cowden	Colden 1250, 1286	Either O.E. *col-denu* = valley where charcoal was burnt, or O.E. *col-denu* = cool valley.
1	Cowgate	Cougate 1290	Probably the range of pasture for a cow – literally where it could go.
3	Cowpen(oo)	Cupum 1175	O.E. and M.E. *cupe* means a basket, in this case used for catching fish.
40	Cragshiel	le Cragscriel 1291	(O.E.) Shiel by the crag (M).
2	Cramlington	Cramlingtuna 1130	M. thinks that the first element might be Cramel – in which case it would mean his people's settlement. Ek. thinks it may be from O.E. *Cranwella*, which means Crane's spring.

6	Craster	Craucestre 1242	O.E. *crawe-ceastre* = old fort inhabited by crows. The Roman association of the name is interesting, as Roman pottery has been found at Dunstanburgh Castle – a much later fortification.
24	Crawley	Crawelawe 1225	O.E. Crow's hill.
4	Cresswell	Kereswell 1234	O.E. Spring where water cress grew.
31	Crookdean	Crokeden 1324	Old Scandinavian *krokr* – O.E. *denu* = the winding (stream) valley.
18	Cronkley	Crombeclyve 1268	O.E. *crumbe-clif* = crooked cliff (M).
36	Crookham	Crucum 1244	O.E. Settlement at the bends (of the River Till).
36	Crookhouse	Le Croukes 1323	The bends (of Beaumont Water).
2	Cullercoats	Culvercoats 1600	O.E. *culfre-cots* = dove cotes.
34	Cushat Law	Cousthotelau 1200	O.E. *cuscote* (dialect cushat) means a wood-pigeon. O.E. *hlaw* = hill. Wood-pigeon hill.
28	Dalton	Dalton 1256	O.E. *dael-tun* = valley farm.
10	Dalton	Dalton 1201	O.E. *dael-tun* = valley farm.
10	Darras Hall	Calverdon Araynis 1242 Calverdon Darreyne 1346	The part of Callerton that belonged to the de Araynis family (from Airaines in Somme). (In 1242 Wydo de Araynis held the manor.)
42	Davyshiel	Davisel 1344	O.E. Davy's shiel (pasture) (M).
21	Deanham	Danum 1198	O.E. *denu-ham* = settlement in the valley; or valleys.
13	Deanmoor	Denemora 1280	O.E. *denu-mor* = fen in the valley.
1	Denton	Dentuna 1252	O.E. *tun* in a valley.
6	Denwick	Denewyck 1242	O.E. *denu-wic* = valley farm.
(18)	Derwent River	Dyrwente 1050	A pre-Roman name that is derived from British derva – "oak". It means a river where there were many oak trees.
26	Detchant	Dichende 1166	O.E. *dic-ende* = the end of the ditch or dyke.
	Devils Water (Tynedale)	Diveles 1230	British *dubo* (black) and Old Welsh *gleis* (stream). A black stream. (E.K.)
9	Dewley	Deuelawe 1251	O.E. dew-hill.
48	Dews Green	Dewegreane 12th century	Dew-green (i.e. green where the dew falls heavily).
29	Dilston	Deuelestune 1172	Settlement on Devil's water.
48	Dingbell Hill	Vingvell Hill 1386	Old Norse *thing-vellir* = fields of assembly (this hill could have reminded a Scandinavian of the assembly hill in his homeland).
40	Dinley	Dunley 1279	Hill-clearing.
2	Dinnington	Donigton 1242	Either O.E. Dunning (a)-*tun*, Dunn's people's settlement, or settlement of the people on the hill (*dun*).

29	Dipton	Depedene 1228	Deep dene.
9	Dissington	Digentun 1160 Discintune 1190 Dicheston 1208 Dicentona 1271	O.E. *dic* is a ditch, moat, or embankment, and the site lies two miles from the Roman wall. M. thinks it may be O.E. *Dicing(a)-tun* = Dica's people's settlement. It is most likely to be the settlement of the people who lived near the ditch.
15	Ditchburn	Dicheburn 1236	O.E. *dic-burna* = stream by a ditch or dike.
36	Doddington	Dodinton 1207	There are two possibilities (i) As Dod Law is nearby the name could come from "dod", meaning "hill". (ii) It could be Dodda's people's settlement (O.E. *Doddingatun.*)
28	Dotland	Dotoland 1160	Dot's land (from Old Danish *Dota* or Old Swedish *Dote*).
46	Downham	Dunum 1186	O.E. *dunum* = at the hills.
15	Doxford	Dochesefford 1230	O.E. Docc's ford.
4	Druridge	Dririg 1243	O.E. Dry ridge, perhaps the ridge of sand-dunes.
30	Dryburn	Drieburn 1182	Stream that soon dries up (M).
37	Duddo	Dudehou 1208	O.E. Dudda's *hoh* (probably the projecting piece of land, or crag).
10	Duddo	Dudden 1242	O.E. Dudda's *denu* (valley).
28	Dukesfield	Dekesfeud 1255	O.E. Ducc's field (M).
6	Dunsheugh	Dunchehou 1310	O.E. Dunn's *hoh* (crag).
30	Duns Moor	Donnismore 1479	Dunn's moor.
6	Dunstan	Dunstan 1242	O.E. *dun-stan* = a hill-stone (rocky hill).
7	Dunstanburgh	Dunstanburgh 1321	O.E. *Dun-stan-burg* = fortification on a rocky hill.
29	Dunstanwood	Dunstanwode 1268	Wood by the rocky hill.
10	Eachwick	Achewic 1160	Either O.E. *aecen-wic*, oaks-farm or O.E. Aeca-*wic*, Aeca's farm. M. gives another alternative O.E. *ece-wic*, a lasting dwelling.
35	Earle	Yherdhill 1242	O.E. *geard* = yard. This means a hill with an enclosure.
53	Earlside (now Foulshields)	Yerlesset 1200	Earl's seat.
2	Earsdon	Erdesdon 1233	O.E. Eanred's or Eored's-*dun* (hill).
4	Earsdon	Erdisduna 1198	O.E. Eanred's or Eored's-*dun* (hill).
16	Easington	Yesington 1242	If the M.E. Yese is the name of the stream, the meaning is the settlement of the dwellers on the Yese.
16	Edderacres	Edredakers 1314	Aethelred's fields (M).
11	Edington	Ydinton 1196	O.E. The *tun* (settlement) of Ida's people.
13	Edlingham (injam)	Eadwulfincham 1050	O.E. *Eadwulfingaham* = Eadwulf's people's homestead.

14	Eglingham (injam)	Ecgwulfincham 1050	O.E. *Ecgwulfingaham* = Ecgwulf's people's homestead.
10	Eland, Little	Parva Elaund 1242	O.E. *ealand* = river island.
16	Elford	Eleford 1256	Either Ella's ford or O.E. *ellern-ford* = elder ford.
33	Elilaw	Ylylawe 1290	O.E. Illa-*hlaw* = Illa's hill.
15	Ellingham (injam)	Ellingeham 1130	O.E. Ella's people's homestead.
4	Ellington	Elingtona 1166	O.E. Ella's people's settlement.
54	Ellishaw (sher)	Illishawe 1254	O.E. Illa-*scaga* = Illa's shaw, copse.
39	Elrington	Elrinton 1229	O.E. *elren-tun* = place of the elder-trees (M. gives it as Aelfhere's farm.)
32	Elsdon	Eledene 1226 Hellesden 1236	O.E. Elli's *denu* (valley) (M. gives it as Aelf's valley.)
1	Elswick (elzik)	Elstwyc 1189 Alsiwic 1204	Aelfsige's *wic* (dwelling, farm).
19	Eltringham (injam)	Heldringeham 1200	O.E. *Aelfhere-ingaham* = Aelfhere's people's homestead.
16	Elwick (elik)	Ellewich 1150	Ella's *wic* (farm).
7	Embleton	Emlesdune 1200, Emlesdone 1212	O.E. *emel-dun*. It could be caterpillar hill, but O.E. Aemele's *dun* (hill) is more likely.
28	Embley	Elmeley 1359	(O.E.) elm-clearing (M).
30	Erring Burn	Eriane 1479	British, related to Welsh *arian* = silver. It means a bright stream.
29	Errington	Erienton 1202	The farm on the Eriane stream.
38	Eshells	Eskeinggeseles 1160	O.W. Scandinavian *eski* = ash tree. O.E. *aesc* = ash tree. A shiel is a hill pasture. Thus hill pasture with the ash trees.
4	Eshott (eshert)	Esseta 1186	O.E. *aesc-sceat* = ash-grove.
25	Eslington	Eslinton 1163	Esla's people's settlement.
28	Espershields	Estberdesheles 1230	East Burntshiel (burnt hut or pasture).
12	Espley	Espeley 1242	Aspen wood.
36	Etal(ee)	Ethale 1232	Either O.E. Eata's *halh* (haugh) or O.E. *ete-halh* = a grazing pasture.
36	Ewart	Ewurthe 1218	O.E. *ea-worth* = enclosure on a river.
3	Ewarts Hill	Heworth 1202	O.E. *ea-worth* = enclosure on a river.
22	Ewesley Burn (oozly)	Oseley 1286	O.E. *osle* = blackbird, *leah* = wood. An alternative is Osa's wood.
44	Fairhaugh	Fairhaluh 1245	(O.E.) Fair haugh.
21	Fairnley	Farniley 1271	O.E. *fearnig-ley* = ferny grove.
7	Fallodon	Falewedune 1233	O.E. fallow hill. O.E. Adj. *fealu* means pale brown or yellow.
29	Fallowfield	Faloufeld 1296	Either O.E. *fealu* = fallow, yellowish (field) or O.E. *fealg* = newly cultivated (field).
22	Fallowlees	Falalee 1388	Either O.E. *fealu* = fallow, yellowish (field) or O.E. *fealg* = newly cultivated (field). *Leah* = grove, open space.

51	Falstone	Faleston 1256	O.E. *fealu* = yellowish or O.E. *fag* = multicoloured. O.E. *stan* = stone.
59	Farglow	Ferglew 1279	Unknown (M).
8	Farne Islands	Farne 730	O.E. *fearn* is a fern. There is nothing to account for this.
*	Farnycleugh (Redesdale)	Farinclou 1250 Farneclogh 1398	O.E. *fearn-cloh* = a ferny cliff.
33	Farnham	Thirnum 1242	O.E. *thirnum-ham* = homestead at the thorn bushes.
1	Fawdon	Faudon 1242	} O.E. *fag-dun* = multi-coloured hill.
24	Fawdon	Faudon 1207	
21	Fawns	Faunes 1256	O.E. *fag-naess* = a multi-coloured ridge.
59	Featherstone	Fetherestanehalg 1204	O.E. *fetherstan* = a cromlech (3 upright stones and a headstone).
37	Felkington	Felkindon 1208	O.E. Feoluca's people's hill possibly.
13	Felton	Feltona 1167	O.E. *feld-tun* = a field farm.
30	Felton Hill	Fyleton 1245	O.E. Fygla's *tun* (settlement).
11	Fencewood	Fencewood 1253	Enclosed wood (M).
27	Fenham	Fennum 1085	O.E. *fenn-homm* = meadow by a fen.
1	Fenham	Fenhu 1256	O.E. *fen-homm* = meadow by a fen.
12	Fenrother	Finrode 1189	O.E. *fin* = a heap of wood. O.E. *roth* = a clearing. It looks as though a large clearing had been made in a wood.
36	Fenton	Fenton 1242	O.E. *fen-tun* = settlement by a fen.
26	Fenwick	Fenwic 1208	O.E. farm by a fen.
2	Fenwick	Fenwic 1242	O.E. farm by a fen.
14	Filbert Haugh	Hilburhalgh 1280	O.E. Hildeburgh's haugh (M).
1	Flatworth	Flaforda 1271	Flat-ford (the Dortwick sand shallows).
7	Fleetham	Fletham 1180	O.E. *fleot-ham* = settlement by an estuary or fleet.
36	Flodden	Floddoun 1517	The name was not given in documents before the battle of Flodden in 1513. It could originally have come from O.E. *flode-dun* = a stream from a hill.
23	Flotterton	Floteweyton 1160	O.E. *flot-weg-tun* = a settlement by the road that went over the river (some sort of raft bridge perhaps).
(11)	Font River	Funt 1200	This is probably a British (pre-Roman) name.
36	Ford	Forda 1224	O.E. ford.
19	Fortherley	Falderle 1208	O.E. *faldere-leah* = sheep folder's meadow.
39	Fourstones	Fourstanys 1236	This could be a cromlech, a line of stones, or boundary stones.

25	Fowberry	Folebir 1242	O.E. *folan-byrig* = burg (fort) where the foals were kept.
33	Foxton Burn	Foxden 1325	Fox valley.
13	Framlington, Long-	Fremelintun 1166	O.E. Framela's people's settlement.
53	Gamelspath	Kenylpethfeld 1380	Gamel is an old Scandinavian personal name, so this was the name given to his path.
12	Garretlee	Gerardesley 1296	Gerard's clearing.
42	Garret Shiels	Gerardscheles 1290	Gerard's shiels.
37	Gatherick	Gateriswyk 1281	Dogwood tree farm (M).
5	Gilden Burn	Gildenes dene 1200	Gildwine's valley (M).
13	Glantlees	Glendeleya 1201 (Ek) Glanteleia 1200 (M)	O.E. *glente* = a look-out hill.
24	Glanton	Glentendon 1186	O.E. *glente* = a look-out hill.
(36)	Glen River	Gleni 730	A British river name from British *glano*, meaning that it was clean, tidy, beautiful, holy.
(36)	Glendale	Grendal 1179	Glen valley.
39	Glendue	Glendew 1239	Welsh *glyn* = valley, *du* = dark.
5	Gloster Hill	Gloucestre 1178	Probably the same as the southern Gloucester. The British *Glevum* means a bright, splendid place. The O.E. *ceaster* is a fort. The finding of a Roman altar stone in this area makes the name an interesting one to historians. Was there a fort in a bright, splendid place?
40	Gofton	Goffedene 1279	(O.E.) Gof's valley (M).
43	Golden Pot	Goldingpot 1230	M. thinks that this is the pot of Golda's people. The pots themselves are blocks of stone hollowed out on top, and were probably guide – or boundary stones.
12	Gorfen Letch	Gorsfen 1270	O.E. *gorst-fenn* = gorse growing on the marsh.
1	Gosforth	Goseford 1166	O.E. *gos(a)-ford* = goose ford.
27	Goswick (gozik)	Gossewic 1202	O.E. *gos(a)-wic* = goose farm.
18	Greymare Hill	Graymere 1307 (M)	*Maere* is a boundary mark.
37	Grindon	Grandon 1208	O.E. *grenan-dun* = green hill.
29	Grottington	Grottendun 1160 (M)	M. says this might be Grotta's people's hill, or O.E. *groten-dun* = sandy hill.
11	Gubeon	Gobyon 1200	The Gobyon or Gubiun family left its name on many manors.
30	Gunnerton	Gunwarton 1170	Gunward's settlement (an Old Norse name).
5	Guyzance	Gynis 1242	Guines was a Norman family name from Guines near Calais.
5	Hadston	Hadeston 1189	O.E. Haeddi's *tun* (farm).
27	Haggerston	Agardeston 1196	Probably an old French personal name from *"hagard"* = wild, strange. O.E. *tun* = farm, settlement.

32	Haining	Hayning 1304	Possibly O.E. *haegen* = an enclosure or grove.
30	Hallington	Halidene 1247	O.E. *halig-denu* = holy valley.
29	Halton	Haulton 1161	The nearby hill was probably O.E. *haw-hyll,* or look-out hill. The meaning would be: the settlement at look-out hill.
49	Haltwhistle	Hautwisel 1240	O.E. *heafod* = hill. O.E. *twisla.* M.E. *twisel* = fork of the river. This means the place where the streams join by the hill.
29	Ham Burn	Hamburne 1225	O.E. *ham-burna* = homestead by the stream.
4	Hanging Leaves	Hengandelley 1262	O.E. *hangra* = a slope. Sloping fields.
15	Hangwell Law	le Hengandewelle 1266	A spring spouting from an overhanging rock.
33	Harbottle	Hirbotle 1220	O.E. *hyra-botl* = hirelings' building. (M. sees this as *here-botl,* an army building.)
35	Harehope (harop)	Harop 1185	O.E. *hara-hop* = Hares' valley.
35	Harelaw	Heyreslawe 1296	O.E. *hara-hlaw.* This (and other places) means "hares' hill".
19	Harlow Hill	Hirlawe 1242	O.E. *her(e)-hlaw* = the mound of the people. This could have been a meeting-place. (M. sees it as army-hill.)
21	Harnham	Harnaham 1242	O.E. *haeren* (or *heren*)*-ham* = a stony, rocky homestead.
	Harpath Sike (Cheviot)	Epprespeth 1304 Erriespeth 1307	O.E. *haerepeth* = a main road.
9	Harsondale	Harestanesden 1255	O.E. *har-stan-denu* = grey stone valley.
21	Hartburn	Herteburne 1198	O.E. *heorot-burne* = stag stream.
3	Hartford (harfod)	Hertford 1198	O.E. stag-ford.
35	Harthope Burn	Herthop 1305	O.E. stag valley stream.
2	Hartley	Hertelawa 1167	O.E. *heorot-hlaw* = stag hill.
58	Hartleyburn	Hertlingburne 1195	The stream of the Hartley people (M).
21	Hartington	Hertweiton 1170	O.E. *heorot-weg-tun* = stagpath farm.
34	Hartside	Hertesheved 1255	O.E. stag's head (land).
22	Harwood House	Harewuda 1155	O.E. hare's wood, or O.E. *harwudu* = grey wood.
28	Harwood Shiel	Harewode 1214	O.E. hare's wood, or O.E. *harwudu* = grey wood.
40	Haughton	Haluton 1177	O.E. *halh-tun* = haugh-settlement.
5	Hauxley	Hauekeslaw 1204	O.E. *Hafoc's* (or hawk's) *hlaw* (mound). If "Hafoc's" is correct, there would probably have been a burial mound here.
31	Hawick	Hawic 1242	O.E. *hea-wic* = a high farm. It could have been a look-out place. (M. thinks that the root could be O.E. *haga* = a haw).

39	Hawden	Hauden 1330	O.E. *haga-denu* = haw-valley.
6	Hawkhill	Hauechil 1178	O.E. *hafoc-hyll* = Hawk hill.
51	Hawkhope (hawk'p)	Haucop 1325	O.E. *hafoc-copp* = Hawk hill.
29	Hawkwell Hall	Hauekeswell 1242	O.E. *hafoc-wella* = hawk's spring or stream.
39	Haydon Bridge	Hayden 1236	O.E. hay valley.
26	Hazelrigg (hezlrig)	Haselrig 1288	O.E. hazel ridge.
13	Hazon	Heisende 1170	O.E. *heges-ende* = the end of the hedge, or O.E. *haeg-sand* which could mean an enclosed piece of sandy land. One meaning thus indicates a boundary, and the other something about the land.
18	Healey	Heley 1268	O.E. *hea-leah* = high clearing.
11	Healey	Heley 1235	O.E. *hea-leah* = high clearing.
23	Healey	Heley 1100	O.E. *hea-leah* = high clearing.
36	Heatherslaw	Hedereslawa 1176	O.E. *heahdeor-hlaw* = stag or deer hill.
32	Heatherwick	Hatherwick 1250	O.E. heather dwelling.
45	Hethpool	Hetpol 1242	Pool under Hetha. (O.E. *haeth* = heath). Great and Little Hetha are hills that are crowned with prehistoric forts.
1	Heaton	Heton 1256	O.E. *hea-tun* = high-settlement.
37	Heaton	Heton 1183	O.E. *hea-tun* = high-settlement.
11	Hebron	Heburn 1242	O.E. *hea-byrgen*. A high burial mound, possibly.
14	Heckley	Hecclive 1242	O.E. *hea-clif* = high cliff, or O.E. *haeth-clif* = heather cliff.
9	Heddon-on-the-Wall	Hedun 1175	O.E. *haeth-dun* = heather hill.
20	Black Heddon	Nigra Heddon 1242	O.E. black heather hill.
9	Heddon East and West	Hidewine 1178 Hydewin del East – West 1242	O.E. Hidda's *winn* = Hidda's pasture.
24	Hedgeley	Hiddesleie 1150	O.E. Hiddi's-*leah* (clearing).
18	Hedley-on-the-Hill	Hedley 1242	O.E. *haeth-leah* = a clearing overgrown with heather. This must have been the fate of much abandoned or overworked land.
14	Heiferlawe	Heforside 1283 Heffordlawe 1346	? heifer hill.
12	Helm	Helm 1255	Possibly O.E. *helm* or Old Norse *hialmr* = helmet, also usedrin the sense of a roofed shelter for cattle.
49	Henshaw	Hedeneschalch 12th century	O.E. Hethin's *halh* or haugh.
25	Hepburn (ebb)	(montem) Hybberndune 1050	O.E. *heah-byrgen* = high barrow. There are prehistoric burial mounds in large numbers in this area.

44	Hepden Burn	Heppeden 1233	O.E. *heop(e)-denu* = Rose-hip valley.
33	Hepple	Hephal 1205	O.E. *heop-halh* = rose-hip haugh.
3	Hepscott	Hebscot 1242	O.E. Hebbi's *cots* (cottages or animal shelters).
*	Hernehouse (Redesdale)	Hirnhous 1398	O.E. *hyrne* = corner, angle. So it is house in the corner of land.
12	Heron's Close	Heyrun 1255	Old French *hairon* = heron (M).
40	Hetherington	Hetherrinton 1291	O.E. Haethere's people's settlement (M). Ek. does not include this.
26	Hetton	Hetton 1163	O.E. *haeth-tun* = dwelling on a heath.
12	Heugh (Eshott-)	Hou 1279	O.E. *hoh* = a ridge or spur.
29	Hexham	Hagustaldes ea 681 Hagustaldes ham 685	*Hagustalt,* Old High German, means the owner of an enclosure, a younger son who had to take land for himself outside the village. This type of land ownership carried with it its own kind of social class. The O.E. *ea* is a river, but the word *ham* – a settlement – replaced it (Ek). It became Hextoldesham in 1188.
10	Higham Dykes	Heyham 13th century	O.E. *heah-ham* = high settlement.
21	Highlaws	Heylaw 1250	O.E. high hill.
11	Highlaws	Heghelawe 1292	O.E. high hill.
14	Hinding Burn and Flat	Henneden -burne, -flat 1275	O.E. *henna-dene* = hen's (or water-fowl) valley.
3	Hirst	Hirst 1242	O.E. *hyrst* = wood, wooded hill.
13	Hitchcroft	Hitchecroft 1445	O.E. Hicca's croft (M)?
14	Hobberlaw, earlier Birtwell	Bertewelle 1296	O.E. *beorhte-wielle* = bright or clear spring. There is no explanation for the later name.
26	Holburn	Hoburn 1250	O.E. *hol(h)* = a deep stream.
17	Holy Island	Healand 1150 Halieland 1195	Its earliest name was *Insula Lindisfarnensis* 730 (see Lindisfarne).
33	Holystone	Halistane 1242	O.E. *halig-stan* = holy stone. It was the site of a Benedictine abbey.
2	Holywell East and West	Halewell 1218	O.E. holy spring.
16	Hoppen	Hopum 1242	O.E. at the valleys.
37	Horncliffe	Hornecliff 1208	Cliff in a *horna* (tongue of land).
19	Horsley	Horseley 1242	O.E. *horsa-leah* = horse pasture.
12	Horsley Long-	Horsleg 1196	O.E. *horsa-leah* = horse pasture.
2	Horton	Horton } 1242	O.E. *horh* (or *horu*) *-tun,* which means a settlement on muddy land.
26	Horton	Horton Turbevill } 1242	
10	Horton	rton } 1242	
9	Houghton	Houcton 1242	O.E. *hoh-tun* = settlement on the spur of a hill.
6	Houghton, Little- and Long-	Houcton Magna Houcton Parva } 1242	O.E. *hoh-tun* = settlement on a spur.

29	Houtley	Holtolaye 1243	O.E. *holh-leah* = hollow clearing or wood. (M. sees it as Holte's clearing.)
29	Howden Dene	Holden 1290	O.E. *holh-denu* = deep valley.
6	Howick	Hewic 1100 Hawic 1230	O.E. *hea-wic* = a high farm.
46	Howtel	Holthal 1202	O.E. *holt-healh* = wooded haugh.
32	Hudspeth	Hodespeth 1252	Hod's path (M).
14	Hulne	Holme 1248 Holyn 1265	O.E. *holegn* = holly.
35	Humbleton Hill	Hameldun 1169	O.E. *hamel-dun* = bare hill. (The original meaning of *hamel* is maimed, or cut off.)
30	Humshaugh	Hounshale 1279	O.E. Hun's haugh.
***56**	Huntland	Hunteland 1177	Hunter's land (M).
25	Ilderton	Ildretona 1125	M.E. *hilder-tun* = elder tree farm. (M. thinks it could be Hild's farm.)
20	Ingoe	Hinghou 1229	O.E. Inga's hill.
24	Ingram	Angerham 1242	O.E. *angr-ham* = grassland settlement or farm. The valley has been farmed throughout prehistoric and later times. No doubt it was well established pasture by the time this name was given.
(59)	Irthing River (-dh-)	Irthing 1169	A pre-Roman river name.
11	Isehaugh	Ineshaulgh 1370 Isehaugh 1456	Either Ine's or Isa's haugh.
(17)	Islandshire	Ealondscire 1107	The shire grouped around Holy Island.
1	Jesmond	Gesemue 1205	The mouth of the Ouse burn. The old name for the Ouse was "Yese", meaning 'gushing'.
*	Karswelleas (Redesdale)	Cressewelle Leghes 1360	Fields by the cress spring (M).
20	Kearsley	Kerneslawe 1245	Cynehere's (or Cenhere's) hill or mound.
48	Keenleyside	Kenleya 1230	Hill by Cena's clearing (M).
29	Keepwick	Kepwike 1279	O.E. Kepe's dwelling (M).
1	Kenton	Kinton 1242	O.E. *cyne-tun* = royal manor.
34	Kidland	Kideland 1271	O.E. Cydda's land.
62	Kielder	Keilder 1326	A British name like the Welsh *caled-dwfr*, which means "violent water".
46	Kilham	Killum 1177	O.E. *cylnum* = at the kilns.
2	Killingworth	Killingwrth 1242	O.E. Cylla's people's farm or settlement.
36	Kimmerston	Kynemereston 1244	O.E. Cynemaer's farm.
49	Kingswood	Kingeswood 1135	O.E. King's wood.
21	Kirkharle	Herle 1177	O.E. *Herela-leah*, or O.E. *herg-leah*. Either Herela's grove or temple-grove.
58	Kirkhaugh	Kyrkhalwe 1254	Haugh with a church.
20	Kirkheaton	Kyrkeheton 1296	The high settlement marked by a church.

10	Kirkley	Crikelawa 1176	British *cruc* – O.E. *hyll* – O.E. *hlaw.* All three elements mean hill.
36	Kirknewton	Niweton in Glendala 1336	O.E. *neowa-tun* = new homestead or village, here distinguished by the church.
31	Kirkwhelpington	Welpinton 1176	O.E. Hwelp's people's settlement. The "church" element was added.
58	Knaresdale (Narz-)	Knaresdal 1254	The valley by Knar (M.E. *Knar* is a rugged rock.)
26	Kyloe	Culeia 1195	O.E. *cy-leah* = cow pasture.
58	Lambley	Lambeleya 1201	O.E. lambs' pasture.
39	Langhope	Langhop 1229	O.E. long valley.
39	Langley	Langeleya 1212	O.E. *lang-leah* = long wood or clearing.
36	Lanton	Langeton 1242	O.E. *lang-tun* = long village or homestead.
41	Leam	Leum 1176	O.E. *leam* or *leum* (from *leah*) = at the groves.
24	Learchild	Levericheheld 1242	O.E. Leofric-*helde* = Leofric's slope.
46	Learmouth	Leuremue 1177	The mouth of the River Lever. (O.E. *laefer* = rush or iris.)
22	Leighton, Green (lie-)	Lytedon 1242	O.E. *leoht-dun* = light hill. (M. gives this as Lihtwine's hill.)
14	Lemmington	Lemetun 1158 Lemechton 1186	O.E. *hleomoc-tun* = brook-lime *tun* (brook-lime is a species of speedwell, Veronica Beccabunga).
6	Lesbury	Lechesbiri 1190	O.E. *laece-burg* = physician's manor (the physician being a "leech").
25	Lilburn	Lilleburn 1170	O.E. Lilla's burn.
28	Lilswood	Lilleswrth } 1233 Lilleswude }	O.E. Lilla's wood.
40	Linacres	Linacres 1279	O.E. *lin-aeceras* = flax fields.
17	Lindisfarne	insula Lindisfarnensis, ecclesia Lindisfaronensis 730 Lindisfarena ea 890	Ek. thinks that the people of Lindisfarne travelled to and from Lindis, the name for North Lincolnshire. He breaks the name up as follows: *Lindisfaran* (travellers)-*eg* (island). Bede's description of "gens Lindisfarorum" suggests a colony.
33	Linsheeles	Lynsheles 1292	Shieling among lime-trees. (M. thinks that it could be the O.E. *lin*-pool instead of *lind* = lime-tree.)
4	Linton	Linttuna 1137	Settlement *(tun)* on the River Lyne.
39	Lipwood	Lipwude 1176	Either O.E. *hliep, hlep-wudu* ("leap" in the sense of a steeply-sloping wood) or O.E. Lippa's wood.
13	Longframlington	Fremelintun 1166	(O.E.) Framela's people's settlement.
12	Longhorsley	Horsleg 1196	O.E. *horsa-leah* = horse pasture.

3	Longhirst (langerst)	Langherst 1200	O.E. Long wood or wooded hill.
21	Longwitton	Witun 1236	O.E. *widu-tun* = wood settlement.
23	Lorbottle	Luuerbotl 1178	O.E. Leofhere's *botl* (building) or Leofwaru's building.
26	Lowick	Lowich 1181	O.E. farm on the River Low. (Dialect "low" is a shallow tidal pool.)
27	Lowlynn	Loulinne 1208	O.E. *hlynn* – a linn – a waterfall or pool on the River Low.
16	Lucker	Lucre 1170	Old Scandinavian *lo-kiarr* is a marsh where the sandpipers go.
26	Lyham	Leum 1242	O.E. *leah-hamm*=grove meadow.
12	Lynch Wood	Linchwiteburne 1200	O.E. *hlinc-wudu* = ridge wood.
(4)	Lyne River	Lina 1050	A British (pre-Roman) river name.
4	Lynemouth	Lymu 1278 (M)	Mouth of the Lyne. (Notice that the spelling Linmouth in Ek. and M. is not that on the 1 inch Ordnance Survey map.)
2	Lysdon	Lidisdene 13th century	Lida's valley (M).
22	Maggleburn (Maglin Burn on 1 inch map)	Macgild 1261	A Celtic river name (M).
(28)	March Burn	Marchenburne 1275	?Merce's people's burn (M).
1	Marden	Merden 1294 (M)	Possibly O.E. *mere-denn* = pasture for mares, or O.E. *mearc-denu* = boundary valley.
2	Mason	Merdisfen 1242	O.E. Maerheard's fen.
20	Matfen	Matefen 1159	O.E. Matta's fen.
11	Meldon	Meldon 1242	O.E. *mael-dun* = hill with a monument or cross.
46	Melkington	Millonden 1425 (M)	Perhaps it was O.E. *mylen-denn* = pasture where the mill was.
49	Melkridge	Melkrige 1279	O.E. *meoluc-hryg* = milk-ridge.
19	Mickley	Michelleie 1190	O.E. *micela-leah* = large clearing.
50	Middleburn	Midelburn 1286	O.E. middle burn (M).
16	Middleton	Middleton 1242	
21	Middleton	Middelton Morel 1242	O.E. *middel-tun* = middle-settlement.
35	Middleton	tres Middleton 1201	
10	Milbourne	Meleburna 1158	O.E. *mylen-burna* = mill stream.
2	Milkhope	Mylkhopeleche 1260	O.E. *meoluc-hop-leche* = a milk (rich pasture) valley with a water course.
1	Milton	Mulliton 1204	O.E. *mylen-tun* = mill farm.
46	Mindrum	Minethrum 1050	From Welsh *"mynydd"*, mountain and O.E. *trum* or *drum* = a ridge. The site is hardly a mountain, but it could denote a high ridge.
11	Mitford	Midford 1196	O.E. *myth-ford* = ford at the junction of streams – in this case of the Font and Wansbeck.
11	Molesdon (Moezd'n)	Molliston 1242	O.E. Moll's or Mul's farm.
32	Monkridge	Munkerich 1250	Monk's ridge.

1	Monkseaton	Seton Monachorum 1380	O.E. *sae-tun* = settlement on the sea belonging to the monks (of Tynemouth).
8	Monkshouse	Broclesmouth 1257 le Monkeshouse ex parte boreali rivuli Broxmouth 1495	From being (O.E.) the estuary of Brocc or Broccel this place became a storehouse for the monks of Farne.
3	Moor, Old and New	Pendemor 1296	Possibly Penda(n)-*mor* = Penda's swamp.
40	Morralee	Moriley 1279	O.E. *moriga(n)-leag* = swampy clearing (M).
22	Moralhirst	Mirihildhyrst 1309	O.E. *myr(i)ge-hylde-hyrst* = pleasant-slope-wood.
3	Morpeth	Morthpath and Morpeth } 1200	Although both Ek. and M. say that this is O.E. *morth-peth,* murder path, most spellings point to fen or moor path.
5	Morwick (morrik)	Morewick 1161	O.E. *mor-wic* = fen-farm.
6	Mosscroft	Musecroft 1269	Mousecroft (M).
18	Mosswood	Moseforth 1378	Ford by the moss (M).
16	Mousen	Mulefen 1167	O.E. Mul's fen.
19	Nafferton	Natferton 1187	Old Norse Nattfari, Old Danish Natfari, O.E. *tun.* Nattfari's settlement.
16	Nanny River	Nauny 1245	A Celtic name (M).
21	Nelson	Nelestune 1196	O.E. Neale's farm (M).
36	Nesbit	Nesebit 1242	O.E. *nese-byht* = a noselike bend.
19	Nesbitt	Nesebite 1242	O.E. a noselike bight (bend).
33	Netherton	Nedertun 1050	O.E. *neothor-tun* = lower farm.
12	Netherwitton	Wittun 1236	O.E. *widu-tun* = (lower) settlement by a wood.
3	Newbiggin-by-the Sea	Niwebiginga 1187	O.E. new building or house.
9	Newbiggin	Neubiging 1242	O.E. new building or house.
28	Newbiggin	Neubyggyng 1378	O.E. new building or house.
46	Newbiggin	Neubiging 1208	O.E. new building or house.
9	Newburn	Neuburna 1121	O.E. new stream (probably it changed course).
39	Newbrough	Nieweburc 1203	O.E. new fort.
1	Newcastle-on-Tyne	Novum Castellum 1130 Nouum Castellum super Tinam 1168	New castle.
15 } **10** }	Newham	(Bamburgh and Morpeth Neuham 1242)	New settlement.
16	Newlands	Neuland 1343	Either newly cleared or newly acquired land.
11	Newminster	Novi Monasterii 1137	New monastery.
15	Newstead	Newstede 1377	New place.
2	Newsham	Neuhusum 1207	O.E. (aet) neowan husum – at the new houses.
36 } **13** } **7** }	Newton	(including Kirknewton, Westnewton,-on-the-Moor-, -by the sea)	New settlement.

25	Newtown	Nova villa super Warneth 1330	New settlement on the Warren Burn.
23	Newtown	Newtown 1248	New settlement.
37	Norham-on-Tweed (Norram)	Northam 1050	O.E. Northern hamlet. Earlier it was recorded in 1000 as "Ubbanford", which means Ubba's ford.
	Northumberland	Northhymbre 867 Northymbralond 895	It meant people who lived north of the Humber, but gradually other regions were given their own names. It is used in its modern sense after c 1100·
40	Nunwick (nunnik)	Nunnewic 1166	Nun's dwelling.
12	Oakhaugh	Akehalgh 1201	O.E. *ac-halh* = oak haugh.
29	Oakwood	Acuudam 1160	O.E. oak wood (M).
10	Ogle	Hoggel 1170	O.E. Ocga(n)-*hyll* = Ocga's hill.
37	Ord	Horde 1196	O.E. *ord* = point or "sword" of land.
42	Otterburn	Oterburn 1217	O.E. otter stream.
31	Ottercops	Altercopes 1265	O.E. *Cop* is a hill, but the nearest to "Alter" is Welsh *"altt"* – a hill also. It could be that nearby "Otterburn" has influenced its form.
1	Ouse Burn	Jhesam, Yese 1293	Either O.E. *geosan* = to gush or O.E. *geose* = a gushing river (Jesmond has a similar root).
20	Ouston	Hulkeleston 1201	O.E. Ulfkell's settlement.
48	Ouston	Ulvestona 1279	O.E. Ulf's or Wulf's *tun* (settlement).
16	Outchester	Ulecestr 1206	O.E. *ule-ceastre* = owl-fort. Roman fort inhabited by owls (thus deserted).
13	Overgrass	Ovegares 1255	O.E. *ofer* = brink or margin. M.E. *gares* = a triangular-shaped field. The site is on a ridge bordering fields.
19	Ovingham (injam)	Ovingeham 1238	O.E. Ofa's people's hamlet.
19	Ovington	Oventhuna 1271	Ofa's people's settlement.
29	Owmers	Ulmeres 1296	O.E. *ule-mersc* = owl marsh (M).
1	Pandon	Pampeden 1177	O.E. Pampi's valley (M).
48	Parmentley	Parmontle 1135	O.E. Pearmain – clearing (M).
46	Paston	Palestun 1176	O.E. Palloc's *tun* (farm).
12	Pauperhaugh (pop-)	Papwirthhalgh 1120	O.E. Papworth's haugh.
3	Pegswood	Peggiswrth 1242	O.E. Pecgs-*worth* = Pecg's enclosure.
44	Philip	Fulhope 1331	O.E. foul valley (M).
11	Pigdon	Pikedenn 1205	O.E. *Pica-denn* = Pica's pasture.
33	Plainfield	Flaynefeld 1272	M. thinks this might be Fleinn's field.
48	Plenmeller	Plenmenewre 1256	Welsh *blaen Moelfre* = top of the bare hill.

2	Plessey	Pleisiz, Pleisetum 1203	Old French *Plaisseis* or *plaissiet* = a park enclosed by a plashed hedge – one made of bent and interwoven branches. The name may have been transferred from France.
14	Plunderburn	Plundenburne 1220	?plum-stream (M).
10	Pont River	Ponte 1269	A derivative of Welsh *pant* – a valley.
10	Ponteland (ee)	Eland 1242 Punteland 1203	O.E. *egland* or *ealand* is an island, or island on a river (perhaps surrounded by marshes) in this case the River Pont.
29	Portgate	Portyate 1269	*Port* – (O.E.) *geat* = gate – gate literally. Watling Street runs through a gate in the Roman Wall
***51**	Powtreuet	Poltrerneth 1325	A pre-Roman name (M).
24	Prendwick	Prendewic, Prendwyc 1242	O.E. Prend's farm.
46	Pressen	Prestfen 1177	O.E. The priest's fen.
15	Preston	Preston 1242	O.E. *preosta-tun* = the priest's settlement.
1	Preston	Prestona 1198	O.E. *preosta-tun* = the priests' settlement.
10	Prestwick (-tik)	Prestwic 1242	O.E. the priests' farm.
9	Prudhoe	Prudho 1173	O.E. Prudha's *hoh* (projecting ridge), or *prud* could mean in a proud position.
33	Puncherton	Pun(t)chardon 1250	Punchardon was the Norman French owner (Pontchardon is in Normandy).
49	Ramshaw	Ramschawes 1312	O.E. *hraefnes-wudu* = raven's wood (M).
53	Ramshope	Rammeshope 1230	O.E. *hramsa-hop* = valley where wild garlic grew (Ek), or O.E. *ramm-hop* = ram valley (M).
15	Ratchwood	Wrethewode 1279	O.E. *wrecca-wudu* = outlaw's wood.
40	Ravensheugh	Ravenshugh 1354	O.E. raven's *hoh.*
31	Ray	Raye 1300	M. says this is either *ray* = darnel or *wray* = landmark. (There is also another possibility: O.E. *aet thaere ea* "at the river" became M.E. *atter e, attere,* and this was wrongly divided as *atte-re*. Thus Re could be taken to be the river.)
32	Raylees	Raleys 1377	O.E. roe-deer clearings (M).
24	Reaveley	Reueley 1242	Either (O.E.) the reeve's clearing, or O.E. *hreof-leah* = rough clearing.
49	Redburn	Redburn 1255	O.E. *hreodburna*=reed-burn (M).
41	Rede River	Rede 1200	O.E. *reade* = the red one.
41	Redesdale (ridz)	Redesdale 1075	The Rede valley.

41	Redeswood	Rode-, Rede-wode 1255	Rede wood.
59	Redpeth	Redepeth 1255	O.E. red or reed path (M).
6	Rennington	Reiningtun 1104	O.E. Regna's people's settlement.
19	Riding	Ryding 1262	O.E. *ryding* = a clearing.
14	Ridlees	Reddeleys 1320	Possibly cleared land (M).
23	Rimside Moor	Rimescid 1268	The modern form of the name is its meaning. It is on the rim of the Millstone Burn.
11	Riplington	Riplingdon 1242 -tone 1251	The settlement of the Riplingas (i.e., perhaps people who lived on a strip of land like a ridge).
22	Ritton	Rittona 1145	O.E. *rith-tun* = settlement on a small stream.
42	Rochester	Roff 1208	Hrofi's Roman fort, or O.E. *hroc* = rook's fort.
7	Rock	Roch 1164, Rok 1242	O.E. *rocc* (from Old French roche and roke). There are outcrops of limestone.
25	Roddam	Rodun 1201	O.E. *rodum* = (at the) clearings (*-rod* meaning clearing, is fairly common in field names).
***1**	Rodestane	Rodestane 1320	O.E. cross-stone (M).
15	Rosebrough	Osberwick 1252	O.E. Osburh's farm (M).
25	Roseden	Russeden 1242	O.E. *rysc-dun* = rush valley.
25	Ross Castle	Rosse 1208	Welsh *rhos* = moor. Irish *ros* is a hillock or promontory. As Ross Castle is both a prominent hillock and on a wide stretch of moorland it could be either, but the "hillock" seems more likely.
23	Rothbury	Routhebiria 1125	O.E. Hrotha's *burg* (fortification) (Ek).
21	Rothley	Ruelea 1195	O.E. Hrotha's *leah* (clearing) (M), or O.E. *roth(u)-leah* (Ek) clearing – open ground. (It is interesting that M. does not use "Hrotha" in the first element of Rothbury, whereas Ek. does – and vice-versa in Rothley).
40	Rouchester	Rowchestre 1348	O.E. rough fortification.
13	Roughley Wood	Ruely 1296	O.E. rough clearing.
44	Rowhope	Ruhope 1233	O.E. rough valley.
9	Rudchester	Rodecastre 1251	O.E. Rudda's *ceaster* or Roman fort.
14	Rugley	Ruggele 1210	O.E. *hrucge-leah* = woodcock meadow. (M. sees this as Rugga's clearing.)
20	Ryal	Ryhill 1242	O.E. rye hill.
24	Ryle	Parva Rihull 1212	O.E. rye hill.
29	St. John Lee	Capella Beati Johannis de Lega 1310	Church of St. John in the clearing.
10	Saltwick	Saltwyc 1268	The place where salt was made (M), or the farm among the sallows?
29	Sandhoe	Sandho 1225	Sand-*hoh* (spur).

1	Sandyford	Sandeforthflat 1384	Sand-ford (or perhaps *sand -eg-ford* = sandy island ford ?)
33	Scrainwood	Scravenwod 1242	O.E. *screawena wudu* = wood of shrewmice or of villains.
27	Scremerston	Schermereton 1196	A manorial name. *Schermer* = *"escrimer"* = fencer (French *'escrimeur'*) (Ek).
6	Seaton	Seyton 1280	O.E. *sae-tun* = homestead by the sea.
3	Seaton North	Seton 1242	O.E. *sae-tun* = homestead by the sea.
2	Seaton Delaval	Seton de la Val 1270	La Val is in Normandy. The settlement by the sea was held by the de la Val family.
2	Seghill	Sihala, Syghal 1198	O.E. *Sige-halh* = haugh on the Sige stream (Ek).
***28**	Sessinghope	Sessynghop 1336	Cissa's valley (M). (Could it, however, be a Normanised form of Seaxingahop ?).
39	Settling Stones	Sadelingstan Sadelestanes 1255	The saddling stones – the place where people mounted their horses.
40	Sewing Shields	Swyinscheles 1279	O.E. Sigewine's shiels.
3	Shadfen	Shaldefen 1257	O.E. *scealde-fen* = shallow fen or fen in a hollow.
21	Shaftoe	Shatfho 1231	O.E. *sceaft-hoh* = a shaft-shaped ridge of land. This description fits the sandstone crags.
33	Sharperton	Scharberton 1242	O.E. *scearpa beorg* = steep hill.
24	Shawdon	Schaheden 1232	O.E. *scaga-denu* = copse valley.
3	Sheepwash	Sepewas 1178	O.E. *sceapwaesce* = sheepwash.
11	Shelly	Shelyngley 1290	O.E. Clearing with a shieling on it.
28	Shield Hall	Schelis 1296	Shiels. M.E. *schele* = a temporary building, a shepherd's hut.
1	Shields, North	Chelis 1268	M.E. *schele* = a temporary hut, a shed, the kind of hut used by a shepherd in summer.
13	Shield Dykes	Swynleys 1288 Swynleysheles 1314 Schelldyke 1538	Swine-clearing, then shiels by the swine-clearing, then a dyke by the shiel. An interesting example of the growth of a place-name.
1	Shieldfield	Schenefeud 1255	Field with shiels or a shieling on it (M).
13	Shilbottle	Siplibotle 1228	O.E. *Scipleaingas-botl* = the Shipley people's building (Ek). (There are other "Shipleys" in the Alnwick area.)
43	Shilmore	Shouelmore 1292	O.E. Scufel's swamp (M).
11	Shilvington	Schilington, -don 1242	O.E. *scylf, scelf* = rock, crag, O.E. *scylfe, scilfe* = ledge, shelf. The settlement of the people at a ledge (Ek), or Scylf(a)'s people's settlement (M).
14	Shipley	Schepley 1236	O.E. *sceap-leah* = sheep-pasture.

40	Shitlington	Sutlingtun 1240	O.E. Scyttels' people's settlement (M).
42	Shittleheugh	Shotelhough 1378	Not clear. It might be Scot's haugh (M).
19	Shoreden Brae	Schortedene 1290	Short valley (M).
8	Shoreston	Schoteston 1177	O.E. Scot's settlement.
37	Shoresworth	Scoreswurthin 1085	O.E. *score* } steep slope *-worth* } enclosure.
21	Shortflatt	Le Scortflat 1284	O.E. short flat or furlong.
18	Shotley	Schotley 1242	O.E. *scotta-leah* = the Scots' clearing.
16	Shotton	Sothune 1196	Scot's settlement (M).
46	Shotton-in-Glendale	Scotadun 1050	Hill of the Scots (Ek).
40	Simonburn	Simundeburn 1229	O.E. Sigmund's stream.
22	Simonside	Simundessete 1279	Sigemund's-*(ge)set* = seat or settlement.
58	Slaggyford	Chaggeford 1218	M.E. *slag* – O.E. *ford.* A ford slippery with mud.
28	Slaley	Slaveleia 1166	O.E. *slaef-leah* = a muddy piece of cleared land.
3	Sleekburn	Sliceburne 1050	Muddy stream (Ek). (Dialect *sleech, slitch, sleek* = mud.) M. attributes this to M.E. *slike* = smooth, but it seems that Ek. is more likely.
51	Smales	Smale 1279	Also Smalesmouth and Smales Burn. From O.E. *smael* = narrow.
51	Snabdaugh (Snapduf)	Snabothalgh 1325	O.E. *snab-halh* = haugh by the little hill (M).
14	Snipe House	Swinleysnepe 1290	Possibly swine-clearing-pasture if O.E. *snaep* is used in the sense of Old Norse *snap* = poor grazing (M).
23	Snitter	Snitere 1176	M.E. *sniteren* = to snow. (Dialect "snitter" is a biting blast.) It could be that the place is named after its cold, exposed position.
13	Snook Bank	Schakelzerdesnoke 1264 Skalkelyerdesnoke 1273	This could be a shackle-yard, where cattle were tied. A "snook" is a sharp-pointed projection, which corresponds with this geographical position.
48	Snope	Suanhope 1325	O.E. Snow-*hop* (valley).
32	Soppit	Sokepeth 1292	O.E. *soc-peth* = a marshy path.
*	Sowerhopeshill (Cheviot)	Suggariple 1050	The location is uncertain, the meaning unknown.
16	Spindleston	Spilestan 1166	O.E. *spinele-stan* = spindestone – a pillar of whinstone, probably, that looked like a spindle.
53	Spithope	Spithope 1324	O.E. A spit-shaped *hop.*
6	Stamford	Staunford 1242	O.E. stony-ford.
20	Stamfordham	Stanfordham 1188	O.E. stony-ford-settlement.
2	Stannington	Stanigton 1242	O.E. *stanweg-tun* = paved-road-settlement.
12	Stanton	Stantuna 1201	O.E. *stan-tun* = stone farm.

39	Staward Peel	Staworth 1215	O.E. *stan-worth* = stone enclosure.
28	Steel	Le Stele 1269	Precipice (dialect "steel" from O.E. *stigol*, which means "stile" but came to mean a steep ascent).
19	Stelling	Stelling 1242	Dialect "stelling" is a cattle fold.
4	Stobswood	Stobbeswod 1250	O.E. *Stobs-wudu* = a wood with tree stumps.
19	Stocksfield	Stokesfeld 1242	O.E. *stoc-feld* = field belonging to the holy place – in this case the monastery.
39	Stonecroft	Stancroft 1175	O.E. Stone-croft.
16	Stotfold	Stotfald, Stodfald 1244	O.E. *stod-fald* = stud fold.
5	Sturton	Stretton 1242	Normally O.E. *straet-tun* = a settlement on a paved road. Most Strettons are on Roman roads. As there is a Gloster Hill in the area, perhaps there is more Roman material to be discovered.
18	Styford	Styfford 1212	O.E. *stig-ford* = path-ford.
41	Sunday Burn	Sunday – burn 1291	—
41	Sundaysight	Sunday heugh 1325	—
7	Sunderland, North	Suthlanda 1177	O.E. *suth-land* = southern land.
16	Swainston	Swayneston 1351	Sveinn's farm (M).
13	Swarland	Swarland 1242	O.E. *swaer, swar-land* = heavy land (i.e., to plough).
31	Sweethope	Swethop 1215	O.E. a sweet, pleasant valley.
30	Swinburn	Swineburn 1236	O.E. swine stream.
7	Swinhoe	Swinhou 1242	O.E. *swin-hoh* = swine-hill.
52	Tarsett	Tyreset 1244	Possibly (O.E.) *Tir-saet* = Tir's field (M).
40	Tecket	Teket 1279	A Celtic name (M).
39	Tedcastle	Tadecastell 1364	Tada's castle (M).
40	Tepper Moor	Tepermore 1479	No explanation.
59	Thirlwall	Thurlewall 1256	O.E. *thyrel* = perforated. A gap in the Roman Wall.
13	Thirston	Thrasfriston 1242	O.E. Thraesfrith's *tun* (settlement) (In Old German place-names the element *thras* and Old Norse *thrasa* means "to threaten" – so in this the person could be nicknamed a pusher or thruster.)
9	Throckley	Trocchelai 1161	O.E. *Throca-hlaw* = Throca's tumulus.
30	Thockrington	Thokerinton 1223	O.E. Thoker's people's settlement.
19	Thornbrough	Thorneburg 1242	O.E. *thorn-burh* = a fort where thorns grew.
49	Thorngrafton	Thorgraveston 1150	O.E. *thorngraf-tun* = thornbrake-settlement.
37	Thornton	Thornetona 1208	O.E. *thorn-tun* = thorn-bush settlement.
21	Thornton, East and West	Torinton 1203	O.E. *thorn-tun* = thorn-bush settlement.
12	Thornyhaugh	Thornihalugh 1309	O.E. a haugh overgrown with thorns.

39	Threepwood	Trepwoode 1308	O.E. *threapian*, M.E. *threpen* = to dispute. Wood of disputed ownership (M).
11	Throphill	Trophill 1166	O.E. *throp-hill* = farm hill.
23	Thropton	Tropton 1177	This might mean the farm at the crossroads (Ek).
23	Thrunton	Trowentona 1180 Torhenton 1199	M. thinks this is Thurwine's farm.
(36)	Till River	Till 1050	A Celtic river name (M). Ek. identifies it with the Tille R. in France. Like the Welsh *tail* and Middle Breton *teil* it could mean "to dissolve, flow".
47	Tillmouth	Tyllemuthe 1050	Mouth of the River Till.
24	Titlington	Tedlintona 1123 Titlingtona 1154	O.E. Titel's people's settlement.
12	Todburn	Totborne 1434	Fox – stream or Tota's stream
48	Todhill	Todholes 1312	M.E. *tod* = fox. Foxholes (M.).
30	Todridge	Todrige 1479	Fox ridge.
5	Togston	Toggesdena 1130	O.E. Tocga's valley.
31	Tone	Tolland 1296	Perhaps O.E. *toln-land* = land on which toll is paid.
23	Tosson	Tosse, Thosse 1150	O.E. *tot-stan* = a look-out stone.
11	Tranwell	Trennewell 1268	Old Norse *trani*-cranes. O.E. *welle*-stream. Crane's stream.
23	Trewhitt	Tirwit 1150	Old Norse *tyri* = dry, resinous wood. O.E. *thwit* (thwaite) = a clearing in a forest.
10	Trewick	Trewyc 1242	O.E. *treo-wic* = tree-farm.
25	Trickley	Trikelton 1177	?sheep dung farm (M).
4	Tritlington	Turthlyngton 1170	O.E. Tyrhtel's people's settlement.
42	Troughend (trufend)	Trocquen 1242	No explanation. Possibly Celtic.
44	Trows	Wytetrowes 1197	White troughs (depressions)? (M).
7	Tughall	Tughala 1104	O.E. Tugga-*healh* = Tugga's haugh.
(27)	Tweed River	Tuidi fluminis 730 Tweoda 1050	A Celtic name, probably meaning "powerful" (Ek).
27	Tweedmouth	Tuedemue 1208	Mouth of the Tweed.
15	Twizel	Tuisele 1208	O.E. *twisla* = the fork of a river.
10	Twizell	Twisle 1050	O.E. twisla = fork of a river.
(1)	Tyne River	Tina 150 Tina, tinus 730	The name probably means "river" derived from *ti* (as in Till), meaning "to dissolve or flow". (Ek). O.E. *thinan* = to dissolve.
(29)	Tynedale	Tindala 1158	Tyne valley.
15	Tyneley	Tyndeley 1278 Tyneley 1663	This looks similar to the Tyne valley but its meaning is not clear.
1	Tynemouth	Tinanmuthe 792	The mouth of the River Tyne.
4	Ulgham (uffm)	Wlacam 1139 Ulweham 1242 Ulcham 1251	O.E. *ule-hwamm* = owl corner (nook).

59	Ulwham	Ulgheham 1479	O.E. *ule-hwamm* = owl corner (nook).
24	Unthank	Unthanc 1207	O.E. *unthances* = without leave (i.e., a squatter's place).
49	Unthank	Unthanc 1200	O.E. *unthances* = without leave (i.e., a squatter's place).
39	Vauce	Vaus 1329	A Norman name.
1	Walker	Waucre 1242	O.E. *wall* – M.E. *kerr* (from Old Scandinavian *kiarr*) wall-marsh. This is the marsh near to the Roman Wall.
29	Wall	Wal 1166	On the Roman Wall.
9	Walbottle	Walbotl 1176	O.E. *botl* (building) on the Roman Wall.
21	Wallington	Walington 1242	W(e)alh's people's settlement.
1	Wallsend	Wallesende 1085	The end of the Roman Wall.
59	Walltown	Waltona 1279	O.E. settlement on the Roman Wall.
30	Walwick	Wallewik 1262	O.E. *wic* (farm) on the Roman Wall.
(3)	Wansbeck River	Wenspic 1137	Perhaps O.E. *waegn-spic* (from Low German *spike*) wagon-brushwood causeway. Bridge that could be crossed by a wagon (Ek). The meaning is by no means proved.
29	Warden (West)	Waredun 1175	O.E. *weard-dun* = watch hill.
15	Warenford	Warneford 1256	O.E. ford on the Warren Burn.
16	Warenton	Warnetham 1209	O.E. homestead on the Warren Burn.
40	Wark	Werke 1279	O.E. *(ge)weorc* = fort.
56	Wark	Werch 1158	*(ge)weorc* = fort.
5	Warkworth	Werceworthe 1050	O.E. *Werce-worthe* = Werce's settlement. There was an abbess of Tynemouth in the 7th century called Werce.
(16)	Warren Burn	Pharned 1050	A British (pre-Roman) river name from British *verno* (Welsh: *gwern*) = alders. It means alder stream.
18	Waskerley	Waskerley 1262	O.E. *waesse-leah* = marsh-clearing.
23	Warton	Wartun 1236	O.E. *weard-tun* = watch-place, lookout-place.
1	Weedslade	Wideslade 1197	O.E. *withig-slaed* = Withy valley (or willow valley).
25	Weetwood	Wetewude 1197	O.E. *waeta-wudu* = wet-wood.
12	Weldon	Welden 1250	O.E. *wielle-denu* = spring-valley.
19	Welton	Walteden 1198	*Welte* (from O.E. *wealt*-unsteady) – *denu*. Twisting valley.
11	Whalton	Walton 1203	O.E. *hwael* (Old Norse *hvall*)-*tun* = hill farm.
39	Wharmley	Quarenley 1279	O.E. *cweorn-leage* = mill-clearing.
2	Wheatridge	Whytrig 1296	O.E. *hwit-hrycg* = white ridge.

5	Whirleyshaws	Qwirlecharr 1350	Very difficult. It might have something to do with a quarry in its first element.
39	Whinnetley	Winteleia 1207	? (M).
34	Whiteburn	Whiteburne 1233	White burn (M).
39	Whitechapel	Whitchapel 1368	White chapel (M).
2	Whitehall	Wytelawe 1250	O.E. white hill.
9	Whitchester	Witcestre 1221	O.E. *wyt-ceaster* = white Roman fort.
48	Whitfield	Witefeld 1254	O.E. white field.
2	Whitley	Wyteleya 1198	O.E. *wyt-leah* = white meadow.
24	Whittingham (injam)	Hwitincham 1050	O.E. Hwita's people's homestead.
20	Whittington Great and Little	Witynton 1233	O.E. Hwita's people's settlement.
13	Whittle	Wythill 1266	O.E. white hill.
19	Whittle	Wythill 1242	O.E. white hill.
23	Whitton	Witton 1228	O.E. Either Hwita's settlement or white farm.
18	Whittonstall	Quictunstal 1242	O.E. *cwichege-tunstall*=quickset hedge – farmstead.
21	Whittonstone	le Whystan 1292	The whetstone (M).
58	Whitwham	le Whitewhom 1317	O.E. *wyt-hwamm* = white-valley or corner.
9	Whorlton	Wheruel-, Wherwelton 1323	O.E. *hwerfel-ton* = settlement by the round hill.
4	Widdrington	Vuderintuna 1160	O.E. Wuduhere's people's settlement.
33	Wilkwood	Wilkewde 1230	O.E. Willoc's wood (M).
49	Willimontswyke	Wilimoteswike 1279	(French name) Willimot's farm (M).
1	Willington	Wilflintun 1085	O.E. Wifel's people's settlement.
44	Windyhaugh	Wyndihege 1200	M.E. *hege* = hedge. Windy hedge – if the M.E. form is to be relied upon instead of "haugh".
12	Wingates	Wyndegates 1208	O.E. *wind-gate* = a pass where the wind blows through.
21	Witton Long	Witun 1236	O.E. *widu-tun*=wood settlement.
12	Witton Nether	Wittun 1236	O.E. *widu-tun*=wood settlement.
41	Woodburn	Wodeburn 1265	Named from the stream coming from the wood.
5	Wooden (woodn)	Wulvesdon 1237 Wolveden 1265	O.E. Wolves' hill (M), or O.E. wolves' valley (Ek).
3	Woodhorn	Wudehorn 1178	O.E. wooded point of land.
35	Wooler	Wulloure 1187 Welloure 1196	O.E. *wella-ofer* = stream-bank.
10	Woolsington (wisintn)	Wlsinton 1204	O.E. Wulfsige's people's settlement.
25	Wooperton	Wepredane 1179	Possibly O.E. *weoh-beorg-denu* temple-hill-valley (Ek).
33	Wreighill (ree)	Werihill, Werghill 1293	O.E. *wearg-hyll* = felon-hill. (Perhaps the place where the felons were executed.)
23	Wreigh Burn (rye)	Rye 1540	O.E. *wearg* = a felon (M).
59	Wydon	Wyden 1255	O.E. wide valley (M).

9	Wylam	Wilum 1198 Wylum 1271	O.E. *wil* is a trick or mechanical device, such as a water mill. The derivation here could be *Wil-hamm,* a water mill on a low-lying meadow by a stream (Ek). M. thinks it is "Wila's homestead".
33	Yardhope	Yerdhopp 1324	Probably the *hop* marked by a yard or enclosure (M).
44	Yarnspath Law	Hernispeth 1233	O.E. *earnes-peth* = eagle's path.
29	Yarridge (jarrige)	Jernerig 1232	O.E. *gearwe-hrycg*=yarrow-grass ridge (M).
41	Yearhaugh	Yarhalgh 1312	Fishery-haugh (M).
36	Yeavering (yevrin) (yivrin)	Adgefrin, Adgebrin 730	Gefrin is the old name of Yeavering Bell, a settlement that was in existence throughout the Roman period. The name comes from Welsh *gafre* – a goat, or a compound containing the word (Ek).
23	Yetlington	Yettlinton 1187	O.E. Geatela's people's settlement.